T0065584

SILENCING
OF THE
SIRENS

SILENCING
OF THE
SIRENS

ADITI DASGUPTA

PARTRIDGE
A Penguin Random House Company

Copyright © 2015 by Aditi Dasgupta.

ISBN:	Hardcover	978-1-4828-4870-0
	Softcover	978-1-4828-4869-4
	eBook	978-1-4828-4868-7

Print information available on the last page.

To order additional copies of this book, contact
Partridge India
000 800 10062 62
orders.india@partridgepublishing.com

www.partridgepublishing.com/india

CONTENTS

ACKNOWLEDGMENTS

I extend my gratitude to Dr Baran Farooqi for her unvarying support and encouragement through the course of my research. Her viable inputs helped me initiate a smooth inquiry. My arguments really expanded and improved under her guidance.

My parents, Krishna Dasgupta and Debasish Dasgupta, have always cared for me in everything that I have ever done but their forbearance during the course of this research has outdone all previous anticipations. Thank you for everything.

Lastly, I would like to thank Nitin, my husband, and my grandfather Late Gopal Chandra Dasgupta for making me what I am today. My research clearly would not have been possible without my grandfather's little dream for me and Nitin's eternal support. This book is dedicated to them.

INTRODUCTION

The world's oldest profession—prostitution—has been largely understood in the contemporary sense. While studying history one comes across several categories within the domain of the female where the term prostitution with its implied characteristic does not quite fit in. This is an attempt to understand the courtesan and her talents by creating a dialogue within the Mughal Era and placing it amongst several other valid courtesan cultures, such as the Japanese geisha and the Greek *hetaira*. Invariably, courtesans have been always represented by their ways of dressing, their artful gestures, and their sensual power. The analysis would explore the conditions that had allowed the courtesan culture to grow and prosper, or caused them to perish. A study of the courtesan way of life has been closely tied to these conditions produced by shifting histories. Therefore, status of the courtesans as the forbearers of artistic traditions giving shape to cultural influences gets occluded by the tendency to focus excessively on their sexuality and, therefore, promiscuousness.

Whether drawn from Greek allusions of women being the half-bird/half-woman creatures who are the "sirens" of the sea or women referred to as sexual objects as instructed in *Kamasutra*, courtesans have always been an ambiguous object of desire who have often intrigued observers within debates, both in the past and in the present.

As professional singers and trained dancers, courtesans in the Mughal Age worked against the grain of mainstream music history that canonized dense classical songs and complex ragas. The arts of courtesans have stirred deeper cultural phenomenon that provide many insights into the Mughal code of conduct. Literature, essays, interviews and autobiographies of courtesans who lived during pre- and post-Mutiny Lucknow do not compile to form a sufficient body of literature even today. Most explorations within this area deal only with individual accounts of their lives that further taper the disciplinary concerns. During the course of my research, what I found lacking was a rigorous courtesan-centric cultural study of the Mughal Age (circa 1800 onward). The cult of the courtesan has, therefore, been treated as a microhistorical encounter within the larger framework of historical events.

Courtesanship was a phenomenon that gave women agency to articulate their selves through artistic exchanges, knowledgeable conversations, and sexual favors to such wealthy patrons as they may think fit. The Greek *hetaira* and the *porne* (literally meaning "to sell"), the Indian *tawaif, ganika, domni,* and *devdasi* have been assigned distinct roles and qualities specific to them within the hierarchy. Therefore, their artistic currency can be understood only within the specific cultural realm measured in terms of sexual and monetary exchange and should not be treated as a universal phenomenon. The courtesan way of life allowed the interface between arts and culture, literary, social, economic, and political elements within the space of the kotha structure that functioned on the basis of pleasure principle. These intersecting spaces cause the courtesan figure to become the culmination of both, pleasure and politics, under one realm that were known for influencing court politics and also acted as a crucial outlet for sexual leisure. Courtesans were a class of women who were different from women born in to the rich classes but they could eventually assume various upper class styles and privileges which they earned from their patrons. With such prowess, the courtesan figure positions herself within complex marginality and also acts as a contradiction to the marriage bed and the matrimonial market. Rather, courtesans have replaced mere reproductive sex that takes place within the familial domain with passionate sex. To quote in support of this argument (as quoted by Martha Gordon and Bonnie

Feldman) Doris Srinivasan says, "Wives were keepers of lineage and courtesans were keepers of culture" (6). Even the undeveloped and "rudimentary" definition of the courtesan was restricted to courtly performances based on the exchange of "gifts" from patrons who were followers of the art. The gifts exchanged among these patrons and the courtesans in the Mughal period consisted of possessions such as gold, jewelleries, or *mohur*s that cannot be considered as a simplistic monetary exchange. It is pertinent to note that tawaifdom (term borrowed from Aram Yardumian's critical review on *My Name is Gauhar Jaan! The Life and Times of a Musician*) did not exist on the basis of token exchange, rather, it was more of a companionship arrangement that the patron sought in the space of the kotha. The Greek term, *hetaira*, too means a male counterpart or a "comrade" or "friend." It is interesting to note that the Greek courtesan culture had also defined a separate category for prostitution that was called *porne*. So also in Rome, prostitution was highly categorized and differentiated from the ways of life of the courtesans, such as Ælicariae, *Amasiae*, *Amatrix*, *Ambubiae*, *Amica*, *Blitidae*, *Busturiae*, *Casuaria*, *Citharistriae*, *Copae*, *Cymbalistriae*, *Delicatae*, *Diobolares*, *Diversorium*, *Doris*, *Famosae*, *Forariae*, *Fornix*, *Gallinae*, *Lupae*, *Lupanaria*, *Meretrix*, *Mimae*, *Noctiluae*, *Nonariae*, *Pergulae*, etc. Despite the invisible moral policing against these systems of "prostitution" these were considered as necessary evil in terms of Puritanism and acknowledged the fact that "well-ordered cities need a brothel" (Jackson, 7). However, a categorical shift within the modern-day discourse can be noticed that merged the enterprise of the courtesanship into a commonplace brothel-like structure. Besides, in the Indian subcontinent, the advent of the nineteenth and the twentieth century Victorian prudishness and the formation of acts such as The Contagious Disease Act that the grain of "sin" and sinning enters the domain.

Texts such as *Umrao Jan Ada*, *Nashtar*, and *Between Clay and Dust* teach us the fact that the Urdu and English linguistics and its translations into other cultures carry within themselves an equal weight of complexity that the figure of the courtesan alone carries individually. This is why irrespective of a number of researches the figure of the courtesan continues to remain elusive to the average individual as it is somehow not knowable and can never be fully fathomed. The current perception of a courtesan is much diluted in terms of a whore-like sensitivity and people often mistake them as commonplace prostitutes or *randi*s that existed in the Mughal era. This is why the question of who can be actually called a courtesan, what authorities and agencies define her, and how is she different from a prostitute remains open to further interrogation in the context of current debates. This study will not attempt a very definitive understanding of the courtesan figure, but it will adopt a close-cropped view for understanding the courtesan culture in the Mughal era. "Always negotiating a complex dynamic, courtesans are forever producing themselves and being reproduced by the fantasies of their consumers. Our work moves between the creations of courtesan's imaginations and imaginings of the courtesan" (Gordon, 8). The presence of this agency of the female is present equally in the realm of its art, reality and fantasy which increases the scope of performativity of the courtesan way of life. Therefore, the basis for further inquiry would be in critically discussing the phenomenon of the courtesan way of life that still beckons us invitingly. This attempt to study the cult of the courtesan through the figure of Umrao Jan Ada will be another attempt to excavate a version of history that might have been probably lost due to changing histories and its interpretations.

Discussing music, dance, poetry, and literature is central to the understanding of the cult of the courtesan and one does find that they are were the most knowledgeable, advanced and informed women of the Mughal era. This gave them the agency to strike intelligent and lofty conversation with the nawabs and even hold literary debates. Such an environment and its upkeep were not possible outside the kotha and inside the familial atmosphere as the women who were married lacked the rich tradition of literature, arts, music, and dance that the courtesans embodied. Therefore, the significance of these artistic practices and traditions in the Mughal reign was handled seriously. The fact that tawaifdom allowed women to enter into the professional domain by excelling in arts and skills also gave them a kind of social and economic privilege that the women within the marriage structure lacked.

THE CHAPTERS

The first chapter marks the life and times of the courtesan Umrao Jan Ada. The second chapter studies the case study of Begum Samru—an empowered courtesan who begins her life as a nautch girl and rises to power—that helps in substantiating the analysis, and the third chapter frees the idea and the cult of tawaifdom from the pejorative use of the word "sirens" and discusses their collapse during the extinction of a culture. Therefore, the first two chapters would engage and disengage with the power structure that empowers and disempowers the courtesan figure during the pre-Mutiny and post-Mutiny phase of Lucknow. While Umrao Jan Ada, the most noted historical-fictional character of the Mughal times, will help us look intimately into the arts of the courtesans and the daily performances of a courtesan's life, Begum

Samru will help in assessing the political valuation of the millennia that helped her sustain and accommodate great political feats. Her ways of successful political functioning might have happened due to her personal circumstances that she faced as a nautch girl and her conditioning in the early life within the kotha.

Courtesans did manipulate gender and class boundaries that were influential both, at a personal level and as a collective whole. In other words, a courtesan was conditioned in the same way as were the others in the profession, but courtesans individually did have their own interests in arts and degrees of excelling within the kotha that increased the stakes of the marketplace. A case study of Begum Samru will be also useful for reviewing the history of the Mughal reign. Courtesans in the eighteenth and nineteenth centuries were prominent symbols of elegance, poise, charm, and women having free sexual agencies. Starting from the East India Company till the early eighteenth century, initial fascination with the courtesans made many British administrators adopt personalized harems. The word courtesan, being a widely used translation of the term tawaif, brings in focus the existence and machinations of the court. The term courtesan, therefore, denotes the significance of women who might not have literally performed in the courts of kings and noblemen but did have strong relations with the nawabs and "'played" with ways of performing at court" (Gordon, 18). Therefore, tawaifdom not only made possible sexual intercourse between men and women but also steered a social and a literary intercourse amongst the tawaifs and the nawabs. This, in one way, does seem to replicate the Petrarchan[1] mode of earthly love and divine and amorous love but with a difference. Here the woman does get the agency to be the subject, the object, the speaker and even the author. Thus, unlike the agency-less woman who is subjected to the confines of marriage, the courtesan figure offers a world of contradictions that open up spaces within profane love and carnal love at its best.

Within the domain of patriarchy, the courtesan model can be also seen as a structure that is used by men to highlight and dramatize their angst or reemphasize their social and economic status. Wealthy patrons and elite nawabs visited kothas for some uninterrupted indulgence in arts and mingle with the "literati" of the Mughal society. Links with the most popular tawaif of the Mughal era was a significant determinant of the social status of men and their high tastes in culture. The more a courtesan was defamed the more it was alluring for the nawabs to be associated with her.

This brings us to the third chapter that engages with the settled belief of defining a woman as a siren. The

---

[1] The Petrarchan concept of love eulogized love that was unattainable. First written by Francesco Petrarch (1304–1374), an Italian humanist, the sonnets (fourteen-line poems) were extremely hyperbolic in nature and represented the woman as an epitome of perfection and attached Muse-like qualities to her.

term siren is used pejoratively and ascribes all elusive and deceptive qualities to the woman. The deathly charm of the sirens is intertwined with her sexually charged persona. The siren is a mythical allusion to half-bird/half-woman creatures that lurk as perils of the sea luring men to rocky cliffs. Deceptive qualities and the excess associated with the term siren have often been conflated with the domain of the female and their receptivity within the phallocentric society. The latter half of the third chapter also problematizes and questions the extinction of nawabi Awadh that was one of the glorious regimes of power in Asia. The study also explores the possibility of the extinction of the courtesan culture that was a notable spectacle of the Mughal era and analyses the contributing factors that erased the courtesan establishments and their traditions from the face of history.

The way of life of the courtesan has always been questioned since the time British colonialism entered the Indian threshold. Later, during the Mutiny of 1857, the colonial propaganda became one of the factors that instigated a rapid melting away of courtesan culture. The first symptom of the British overpowering was the disempowerment of the Plutocratic class of the nawabs. Consequently, the fading of the "economics of patronage" (Gordon, 23) led to the destabilization of the consumers of the arts produced by the courtesans. The courtesans, therefore, voyaged from the center of the spectacle to the margins of a fading culture by the end of the twentieth century. Around the 1950s, all centers of music and other classical singing traditions run by the courtesans of Lucknow were drastically shut due to commercialization of music[2]. All India Radio did away with all the women singers and therefore, the agency of the kotha and the courtesans were withdrawn by force.

> In their drive against nautch, the missionaries were now joined by a powerful group of educated Indian social reformers who, influenced by Western ideas and Victorian moral values, had lost pride in their own cultural heritage. In 1892, they started an "anti-nautch" movement at Madras which spread to other parts of the country. (Nevile, 115)

This movement gained momentum with the support of the active press and various associations and clubs were set in the society to monitor and stop nautch performances in the city. This continued till the 1930s when All India Radio's decision to boycott all women singers acted as a deathblow to stop all mehfils and "rescue it (society)

---

2   This is when the Anti-Nautch Movement took place started by the emerging bourgeoisie class that was highly influenced by Western ideas of culture and dressing. The institution of the nautch and the *mehfil* came under heavy attack of moral issues and anti-Christian feelings (as propagated by the British).

from the clutches of the 'infamous' tawaifs and devdasis" (Nevile, 124).

Therefore, it is observed that with the dissolving of Plutocracy, annexation of Awadh and the emergence of the middle class in the twentieth century consequently gave rise to the biggest contradiction of the time: "a middle-class respectable married woman and a 'connoisseur' of Indian music" (Gordon, 24). If the elite social and economic structure of the Mughals had to disintegrate and reappear as the middle class in several parts of northern India, then it also sees the homogenous culture of the courtesans disintegrate into heavily loaded terms, such as the middle class, respectablility, and marriage. The consumption of art did not undergo a sea change but the means of producing it did. Music and dance were performance oriented, and operated on the principles of gestures, performativity and enactment. With the production of Shellac records and mushrooming of recording studios, art was definitely meant to diversify from the hands of concentrated elite and patrons of art to the masses who were the new class of potential consumers.

The concluding chapter ties arguments together. It juxtaposes Lucknowi tawaif culture along with the Japanese courtesan and geisha culture, and highlights reasons that sustain the latter even today. The survival of the Japanese geisha model and its validity even today might be a possible cultural clarification to the "unspeakable professions" of India.

Works Cited

Feldman, Martha and Bonnie Gordon. *The Courtesan's Arts: Cross-cultural Perspectives*. USA: Oxford University Press, 2006.

Jackson, Brian L. "The Harem Syndrome.' PARRC Research, Inc. 2006. Web. 30 May 2012. <http://www.pdfnow.net/pdf/the-harem-syndrome.html>.

Neville, Pran. *Nautch Girls of the Raj*. Delhi: Penguin, 2009.

Sampath, Vikram. *"My Name is Gauhar Jaan!" The Life and Times of a Musician*. New Delhi: Rupa, 2010.

CHAPTER ONE

THE (DIS)EMPOWERED WOMAN

A highly sequestered place, engrossing, with women dressed magnificently; bejewelled in precious stones and jewelry, her couplets sound convincing and declare her presence instantly. The listeners sit dumbfounded by her beauty and her charm. She claims and denies in the same tone, communicating a shared secret to her patron. She attracts her audience to keep watching—these being the opening moments of a mehfil held inside seraglios of royal princes.

It has been over 116 years since *Umrao Jan Ada* (1899) was published in Urdu. By now, some of the ambiguity surrounding Umrao's historical fictional presence has encouraged many stereotypical images of the figure of the

1

courtesan. Scholarly volumes have discussed the emergence of the cult of the courtesan and its disappearance with the end of the Mughal Empire. Most of the available (i.e., published) material seem to focus on biographical details of courtesans or elaborate on highly romanticized images of the courtesan figure. However, some of the existing textual accounts that discuss the figure of courtesan, focussed primarily on the life of Muslim women, such accounts show influence of European accounts of Mughal self-indulgence and treachery. Later day works on life, art and the origin of courtesans have been undertaken by Abdul Halim Sharar, Shamsur Rehman Farooqi, Pran Neville, K. S. Lal, Veena Talwar Oldenburg, Abraham Eraly, Durba Ghosh, R. Nath and others who have produced studies of the courtesan figure in a more complex manner, engaging with people and their culture elucidating factors that sustained the way of life of the courtesan.

However, the question still remains—even though the figure of the courtesan has been contextualized and legitimized within current debates, what allowed her to walk the corridors of power permits further discussion. Besides, history of Lucknow is incomplete without the mention of courtesan culture which, however, is replete with conflicting attitudes from its contemporary as well as later generations. Therefore, understanding the cult of the courtesan is relevant for untangling some of the problems associated with it. Efforts will be made to analyze them individually against otherwise stereotypical interpretations. The attempt is to trace some borrowings from the traditional approach, rationalize the level and the context of such approaches, and revisit the cult of the courtesan that has been denied a specific space of thought.

The representation of courtesans has played a major role in the formulation of myths and fictional narratives in post-Mutiny Lucknow. In spite of a debatable portrayal of the courtesan culture, what makes the study contemporary? Lives of courtesans may be easy to chronicle but it is important to be aware of the deep and the complex dynamics of economic, moral, and cultural forces governing the courtesan way of life. A visible crystallization of stereotypical ideas has taken place even before one begins to understand the nuances of the cult of the courtesan. Several accounts written by the Europeans also talk about the excesses which, according to them, this culture was responsible for. It remains for the researcher to assess whether this culture faded away because of the inherent flaws of debauchery and decadence or was it yet another victim of the policy of the foreign race that had no insight into the models of existence and livelihood that existed outside Europe? Of course, the plurality of models of domesticity and race was something it just could not fathom.

If the global historical culture is taken into account, then precolonial India, ancient Greece, and Edo Japan have witnessed the culture of courtesans much more distinctly than other countries. Attempts have been made by several critics to explore the fading out of the tawaifdom. Many literatures that discuss the courtesan culture in Greece, Japan, Rome, and India have, therefore, surfaced in the last few years. However, these cultures are still being studied for their existence, what made them flourish and what factors were responsible for their decay. The attempt would be to historically locate and analyse this tawaifdom[3] individually lifting specific examples from Greece and comparing conditions there with conditions that allowed the production of a text like *Umrao Jan Ada* in India. This analysis will consider three important factors: the courtesan's empowerment, their dis-empowerment, veiled ironies and their lifestyle. Also, Umrao's upbringing within the kotha culture and what makes her the personification of an indispensable Mughal courtesan will be studied closely with respect to the prospering culture of the Mughals in India. Muhammad Hadi Ruswa's *Umrao Jan Ada* was published in 1899 and its first translation in English was done only in the year 1996. Umrao Jan, portrayed as an extremely cultured courtesan, becomes infamously famous as she brings forth a lot of scepticism along with her powerful and memorable existence. It can be said that a phenomenon was born and the making and remaking of the courtesan figure into films only added to its intensity and breathed new life into the treatment of the subject. One can find similar traces of the making of a powerful courtesan in

---

3   Term taken from <http://www.timesquotidian.com/2010/11/20/gone-in-the-air/>.

Hasan Shah's *Nashtar* (1790) that was published almost hundred years before *Umrao Jan Ada*. Vinay Lal, in his essay, "The Courtesan and the Indian Novel" states:

> Hasan Shah was, as he himself says, a man of respectable even noble birth, although the family's fortunes had suffered somewhat in the political turmoil following the invasions of Nadir Shah and Ahmad Shah Abdali, the Rohilla and Sikh wars, and the decline of the Mughal empire. (Lal, 2)

According to the existing Urdu literary traditions in the 1790s, Lal also outlines the success of Hasan Shah's *Nashtar*. The 1700s saw use of the *masnavi* tradition that used idioms and expressions of love and the pain associated with it. But this had a confessional tone to it in general. *Nashtar*'s sensational success went far above the confessional mode which made the novel

> an arresting work, in the first instance, is the mode in which it is written. The boat journey which Hasan Shah takes to join his wife is the flight of one soul in search of a like soul, the journey of the lover in search of the beloved, and as we know from the use of such imagery in bhakti poetry, a journey of this kind is fraught with hazards: the sea can be stormy, the navigator may be unskilled, the boat may

5

> sink from a leak; and when at all the boat appears to have reached the shore safely, at the very last moment it hits a rock. The path of love is just as tortuous as the road to God. All this is there, one might say, in *The Nautch Girl*, but Hasan Shah invests his account of the journey with fictional devices that have a most poignant effect. (Lal, 3)

Therefore, it can be deduced that *Nashtar* acted as a literary appetizer. In *Nashtar*, the figure of Khanum Jan is central to the novel that primarily beholds the historical interest narrating to us a story of an ill-starred nautch girl Khanum Jan who falls in love with another dancer from the troupe. The theme of an endless wait and unfulfilled love is central to the novel. This novel, therefore, somewhat establishes the basic features of the life of a courtesan but is not really as successful as Ruswa's *Umrao Jan Ada*.

Umrao Jan Ada's life chronicles with her abduction which in a way liberates her. The conventional nature of domesticity would not have made Umrao Jan what she becomes in her life. Ameeran is, therefore, significantly less powerful than the later evolved doppelganger Umrao Jan Ada. The *Oxford English Dictionary* describes a doppelganger as a "ghostly double of a living person, especially one that haunts its fleshy counterpart." One can say that Ameeran remains the subdued mirror image of Umrao, whom the reader forgets right after Umrao begins her journey. Therefore, this rebirth, as I would like to call it, makes it possible for Ruswa to create shades of grey and involve obscurity that would have failed to find its way in a rather naive existence of Ameeran. Ameeran is commonplace; Umrao is extraordinary. Therefore, the figure of Ameeran is least likely to be the culmination of the tumultuous Awadh and the post-Mutiny ruptured sociocultural space; Umrao is more like a response to the cultural erosion that takes place during the siege of Lucknow. Through Umrao, Ruswa presents to us the dismantling of the rich Indo-Muslim Awadh culture which has taken a severe beating as a result of the British Raj. However, the irony heightens when we see Umrao battling with her conscious sensitivity that traps her liberation. We see this in an instance from the text when she visits her natal home during one of her performances. This brings out the split that she has nurtured for long. A woman conscious of being a courtesan and leading a luxurious life still dreams of meeting her mother and secretly longs for that social acceptance—this insight makes the interpretation of Umrao Jan's life exhaustive and caught in a sort of "ritualized prostitution" which makes her neither this nor that (Sahni, 16) and limits her powers to a great extent. A similar incident can be seen in *Between Clay and Dust*[4] where Gohar Jan laments the

---

4   *Between Clay and Dust* is Musharraf Ali Farooqi's latest novel released in 2012. The plot beautifully intertwines the lives of two people who are caught in two dying

7

loss of her performances as she shuts the kotha down due to the Mutiny.

> Gohar Jan had been unprepared for the possibility of the kotha closing down because it had come about through a series of unforeseeable circumstances.... Like waking from a dream broken in disquiet, she was unable to ward off her feeling of despair at the snapping of the thread that connected her past, present and future. She felt restive and disoriented.... It seemed that the kotha had a secret life of its own that was extinguished when she closed its doors. (Farooqi, 74–75)

Gohar Jan is detached from her daughter-like figure Malka and she is aware of the fact that falling in love with her patrons is not an option for her. With Umrao Jan and Farooqi's Gohar Jan, the tone of their confession has a note of regret for the dying culture yet it does not mean that they are ratifying the Indian domesticity and customs of marriage. As the twentieth century set in, a later-stage development was the middle class concept of

---

professions—wrestling and courtesanship. Gohar Jan and Ustad Ramzi are placed at the twilight of their professions and their lives. Their followers have melted away and find that they face the greatest challenges in the personal front.

the *bhadramahila*[5] emerged. There was a felt-need and a visible enthusiasm for concepts such as nationalism, reformation and steps were taken to "cleanse" the society from the clutches of the *ayiaash*. Mary Poovey in her book *The Proper Lady and the Woman Writer: Ideology as Style in the Works of Mary Wollstonecraft, Mary Shelley and Jane Austen* (cited in Tharu and Lalita) discusses:

> One of the tasks the social reform movement set itself…was to break this unregimented and indecorous intercourse between women of all classes and create the respectable middle-class housewife, the *bhadramahila*. The purity and domestic virtue of this newly created being was defined by setting it up as the antithesis of the "unbridled movement" and the "licentiousness" of the Vaishnava poets. For

---

5   "In the nineteenth century, the self-image and the world view of the Bengali middle class were largely shaped by an idea that the society in Bengal was broadly divided between *bhadralok* and *abhadralok*. The *bhadralok* considered themselves as important social agents for modernizing society, politics, religion, education and culture along with publishing newspapers, magazines and literary societies" (Bankim, xxvi–xxvii). This plurality of experience and restrictions placed on women even within the confines of "home" in the Indian context questions and exposes the hypocrisy of the *bhadralok* model.

> women it was a double-edged process, for as this popular culture was discredited and the artists reduced to penury and often forced into prostitution, the new respectable upper-class woman was shaped, her sexuality elaborated, and in the process also contained…. On the other hand, prostitution was spreading like plague in Calcutta. (Tharu and Lalitha, 155–56)

Keeping in mind the model of the *bhadramahila*, Umrao seems as a predated figure that symptomatizes this degeneration that the early twentieth century sees. This model seems to be a standardized version of modernity settling into society and a concept formed under the incubation of the British Raj.

> In the process, a changing and heterogeneous society, with conventions, law, legal institutions, and ideological formations that embodied the different historical experiences of its people, was reconstituted and confined not only by the law but also by the whole range of social practices that took their cue from legal procedure, into stunted upper class image…. As a result, women's "individuality," their "citizenship," and their "freedom" were defined and contained in the domain of the personal not only by the law but also

in the agitated debates on other issues that accompanied the setting up of the law. But as many of the texts that follow show, the personal domain, newly constituted in exclusively religious terms, had complex and problematic connections with caste, tradition, Victorian norms of feminine propriety, and imperialist ambitions. (Tharu and Lalita, 158)

The prudish mind-set borrowed from the Victorian model was setting in by the 1900s, the same time around *Umrao Jan Ada* was published preaching the importance of correct moral views and its presence in society. In this extract, Tharu and Lalitha introduce important viewpoints such as the reconstitution of people under changing historical experiences that also called for change in the social practices and attitudes, and, the introduction and establishment of "individuality" and "citizenship" with the setting up of law. These two points do become a point of reference in our discussion. The displaced identity of a courtesan and the laws introduced to revise the moral values of society modified the role of an individual and most importantly, the role of women within a "reformed" society. The law did bring into action an "ordered" society but it also compartmentalized women into areas or ideas that approved of a "decent" existence.

Regulated by Queen Victoria in Great Britain (1837–1901), the nineteenth century was infested by codes of conduct for women conducting themselves sexually. Several other aspects of Victorian prudishness were attitudes of elitism, low tolerance towards crime and religion and industrialism which were pervading the society. At this juncture in history, the overarching presence and the setting up of the British Empire in India made these values spread in Northern India. The reason for it being called prudish is because, on one hand, codes of conducting the self in society "normalized" the process of cohabiting peacefully in society, on the other hand, prostitution and child labor formed the undercurrents of the society in Britain. Queen Victoria laid excessive importance on specific value systems for what was idealized as a decent living, which included dignity and restraint. Such a strict set of moral codes helped a false consciousness permeate the society. Morality was treated as a straitjacket phenomena that designed the way language should be used publicly, the attire for public appearances and the "language of flowers" was introduced in place of expression of direct sexual feelings. This worked against individualism and could be held responsible for causing a split within the British society. The British colonial project made them apply this one-size-fits-all idea to Indian sensibilities and ban all trades that involved the use of flesh and bodies.

One can say that British culture which was so monolithic and unidirectional was not able to encompass the Indian beliefs of diversity. The Mughal rule in India was diverse and accommodated the native European cultural space with ease. The thriving sociocultural space during the Mughal reign was so rich and plural that British sentimentality could have potentially suffered at the hands of the Mughal kings in India if it had not been curbed by the Britishers. Umrao Jan was one such grand representative of culture in Awadh and the possible indulgences of the Age could have been the next best reason for its extinction, if the British Raj had not taken over. The status of a courtesan was considered as an asset to this *kaghazi raj*[6]. The courtesan could not fall in love as the conventions of the kotha went but the colonial interruption acts as a more far-reaching contributory factor due to which Umrao's character in the novel, and many others who lived outside the text, were bid an untimely farewell.

The power structures (social, political, and cultural factors) that constitute the making of Umrao Jan Ada are some of the most important focal points that need

---

[6] Term borrowed from Abraham Eraly's *The Mughal World*. Eraly rightly assigns the term *kaghazi raj* to the Mughal reign in India and calls it the paper government (p. 231). Eraly goes on to state, "From the reign of Akbar on, copies of all state communications were systematically preserved, along with a vast number of records and accounts, and the daily log of all that the emperor said and did.... Unfortunately almost all of it was lost in the chaos of the eighteenth century, leaving only fragments in the provincial archives."

to be considered for understanding the power structures of the courtesan figure. The novel is written at the brink of the misgovernance of Awadh—a state where the administration is visibly a failure during the 1890s and the crime and corruption rate is overwhelming. At this point in time, the British annexation remains as the only counter-demand of the nineteenth century. The "reasonable" claim of rescuing the state from the clutches of decadence and indulgence seemed a valid enough reason and made the British agitation even more severe. In 1857, Awadh was finally annexed which has been the most protracted rebellion lasting from 1857–59. Post the insurgency began the policy of supporting Hindu zamindars instead of the old Muslim elite. The scene of annexation neared its climax when the Britishers started felicitating the Indian zamindars and landlords with titles and gained more loyalists. This makes Lucknow one of the brilliant examples of state formation in the nineteenth century. Such was the embedded power play that the nawabs of Awadh lost their complete sovereignty and were reduced into a dependant parasitical class of elite which subsisted on pleasure. This is furthered and strengthened in several accounts written by the British making the nawabi Awadh a class entrapped in false consciousness. This Plutocratic[7] class, in short, can be

---

[7] Plutocracy is referred to as a small number of extremely wealthy individuals who control the countries and hold them in ransom. 'Plutocracy' replaced 'democracy' and

defined as the class that is the descendant of the nobility and has given over to a life of consumption. *Umrao Jan Ada* takes shape in this transitional phase. With a complex narrative structure, the novel has two narrators who blur each other's narratives at different points in time. The uniqueness of the novel reflects in this dual narrative pattern that augment the power Umrao enjoys. It is not a linear narrative but a backward one. In the end, is the beginning. It looks back at the beginning of time through a sense of reminiscence. The time of the Self which is enjoyed by Umrao Jan, both in her childhood and as a courtesan, is carefully lodged in between the historical time. As one sees, this personal time is not accessible to Ruswa himself. This personal time foregrounds itself making the historical time play in the background of the novel. As readers we are launched in the midst of power play as the stronger personality of Umrao Jan Ada unfolds itself before us.

Umrao Jan is shown to have already crossed two thresholds in the novel—her childhood and her status as an aging courtesan. This constructs the novel into four essential stages:

'capitalism' as the principal fascist term for the United States and Great Britain during the Second World War." In other words, we can define it as the near-suicidal cult of excesses heading toward its own decline. (http://en.wikipedia.org/wiki/Plutocracy [last visited on 23 March 2012])

1. The pre-Dilawar Khan abduction period
2. Ameeran as a child, growing up in Khanum's house
3. Umrao Jan as a courtesan, and
4. The time of reminiscence

A very brief history that traces the kotha culture in India will be useful in understanding the psyche of the Mughal tradition. Awadh's lenience towards the kotha culture is necessary to the understanding of the courtesan way of life. Babur (1526–1530), the first emperor of Awadh, gave out specific details of the female presence in the house and several other references to his Begums in *Babur Nama*. Humayun's harem (1530–1556) seemed to have institutionalized this culture within the royalty as the *Humayun Nama* discusses Gulbadan as the in-charge of the harem and other descriptions that discussed the candour atmosphere that prevailed inside the harem. With Akbar (1556-1605), the harem culture expanded manifold and his marriages to Indian princesses for geographical expansion and the building of the harem was popular. Jahangir (1605-1627) was the master of his own harem and therefore his records are treated as authentic and highly informative. He was known for his ill health and gave his life up in excessive drinking. As K. S. Lal states in *The Mughal Harem*, "No other writer residing in the harem, narrates such copious information about the Mughal seraglio as Jahangir" (3). During Shahjahan's reign (1627–58), the harem culture was reportedly changed.

> It becomes a very bright and brilliant place and its charm is brought into focus by Persian chroniclers like Qazwini and Abdul Hamid Lahori. During the reign of Aurangzeb certain restrictions were imposed on the harem activities of harem inmates... The activities of the harem-inmates, their wealth, their *jagirs,* their buildings, their gardens, their *jashns,* even their romances, all became exceedingly absorbing and met with excellent treatment at the hands of Persian chroniclers. (Lal, K. S., 4)

Thereafter, Nicholao Manucci's detailed accounts on the harem culture served as great historical documents. Post this, the later nawabs of Awadh expanded the space of the harem and introduced an easy exchange of information that operated within the kotha and the ruling nawabs of the state. Women figures like Jahanara and Roshanara Begum, the daughters of Shah Jahan, and Nur Jahan were women who dealt with politics of the state that one can trace in the history of Awadh.

Mujra was an integral part of the tawaif's performance that originated under Emperor Jahangir and flourished under Emperor Shah Jahan. Mujra which was practised in courts as one of the prime recreations of an Emperor, it slowly found a structure of the kotha where regular performances of the mujra could be held.

> Originally operating from mobile encampments, *tawaif* women were members of organized troupes that would create a settlement to occupy during the time that one of them had a patron. This system can be considered as a temporary relationship between a wealthy older man and a *tawaif*. When North Indian cities such as Lucknow and Kanpur became centers of Mughal power, *tawaif* began to attach themselves to courts and also establish permanent settlements in which to perform their art. (Dewey, 147)

The twentieth century saw the emergence of the word "national reformer" that occurs in the novel during the reign of Amjad Ali Shah and Wajid Ali Shah (Ruswa, 39), which is used in the context of British rule and not under the Indian Presidency. Reformers appeared in good numbers within the Muslim sphere, in India, just as they were appearing in the Hindus. Nazir Ahmad, Syed Ahmad Khan, Ashraf Ali Thanawi to name a few emphasized more on the education of Muslim women. It is here that we get a deeper insight into the growing presence of women in courts, harems, and mehfils and their ability to influence decisions of nawabs and kings. Umrao Jan's life and her interest towards higher education, which she would not have been able to acquire as Ameeran, show the cultural possibilities and academic liberation that a courtesan could have to achieve political feats. Therefore, this novel can be actually seen as a maverick novel because it foregrounds the establishment of the modern woman. Let us discuss this particular conversation between Umrao Jan and Ruswa from the novel that holds prime importance to the discussion:

> Higher class prostitutes don't sing bawdy songs any more in Lucknow. That's the job of *domnis*, though prostitutes have to sing them in villages, even in male company. But whether in the town or in the country, I still don't think that it's a good custom.
>
> Well, it's not bad just because you say so. I've seen with my own eyes just how much pleasure the most upright nobles of our society get out of slipping into the women's quarters and hearing these songs. They listen to their mothers and sisters, and grin from ear to ear. I sometimes wish we had never lived to see this day. And not to mention the scurrilous things that the most respectable ladies sing on wedding nights and the morning after. Still, let's leave this topic and get on with the story. I'm no national reformer to criticise these things! (Ruswa, 39)

The minutia of the life of a tawaif is of no concern to the progressive Muslim. This is where the brilliancy of the Ruswa-nian narrative lies—unpacking Umrao Jan in plutocracy. We see a three-tier transformation in Umrao: Umrao's disempowered childhood, empowered as Umrao Jan Ada and Umrao speaking about being "Ruswa" (disgraced) within her profession. Bringing into focus the life of a tawaif empowers Umrao naturally but what sustains her power is the entire school of thought that Lucknow possessed before the Mutiny. Her fight between her lost childhood and her acquired extravagant existence becomes the culmination of the (dis)empowered woman. One still wonders whether the wealthy, knowledgeable, skilled and popular courtesan was actually empowered or not. Does her yearning for leading a married life not make her dis-empowered? We see how intensely a moral text that highlights the hypocrisy of patriarchy and ways in which men become the agencies of change in a woman's life, yet it does not moralize on the so-called illegitimacy of tawaifdom.

Framed by a certain literary transaction, Umrao's *ada* excels in poetry, grace and civility. When Ruswa asks Umrao to come and join the musha'irah, she fears being recognized. So, we see that a courtesan too is framed and bound within the limits of *adab*[8]. If one compares the case

---

8   Much has been written on adab and scholars have argued that the emergence of the courtly love tradition in the thirteenth and the fourteenth century Europe might have originated from the Persian influence. Lucknow had the Shi'a adab. Adab as a tradition therefore, traveled both East and West and the Eastern reincarnation of culture

of Umrao with that of other women writers appearing in other regional works and talking about their life histories during the nineteenth century (such as Pandita Ramabai, Ramabai Ranade), the story of Umrao Jan Ada can be positioned somewhere adjacent to them in terms of their prominent voice, in depth knowledge of literature and their attempts to transgress the social norms placed by the patriarchy.

This empowered positioning of Umrao Jan Ada can be placed parallely with the figure of the *hetaira*, *porne*, whore, randi, and the domnis. This Greek classification of prostitution was associated with the royalty and elitism. Placing this in the context of Umrao Jan, although these terms were not favourably described, they certainly had positive connotations due to its connection with archaic aristocratic use. Men and women, who practiced this trade, redefined themselves in the archaic period and went on to apply itself in the modern period as well. However, the only difference was that it has now become highly pejorative in its usage.

Courtesans were a class of women who have been called by different names at different points of time in history and civilization. The time that has elapsed from women being devdasis[9] (servants of God) to nartakis to randis can be studied for further clarity.

---

of adab is to be found in Urdu. It still is one of the major protocols of Urdu poetry.

[9]   India during its Medieval Age (around eleventh and twelfth

Even if we consider a sketch in nude, the identity of the woman is something that cannot be ascertained. There is nothing in it to suggest that she is a prostitute, but there is nothing to suggest otherwise. Yet, in most cases, one would argue fervently of how she is a "normal" woman, far from being a prostitute. This denial of space even within the spheres of sexuality is perhaps the most poignant of ironies, as if sexuality by itself is a mainstream attribute. For someone who derives her livelihood through the exhibition of her sexuality, this is denying the very reason of her existence. But her denigration has only begun. (Sahni, 13)

Understanding sexuality has been under the scathing eye for long and it has been more intriguing when it comes to understanding it in the light of defining sexual terms and related gender theories as they are today. Christopher A. Faraone and Laura K. MCclure's *Prostitutes and*

---

century), even before the institution of the courtesans was established, had the prominent culture of *devdasi*s. This *pratha* branched out of the socioeconomic structure of the time and was based on temple worshipping. They too, had a hierarchical structure to follow that was managed by the temple management. This culture vapourised with the arrival of Turkish and Muslim rulers.

Courtesans in the Ancient World provide a wonderful and a detailed insight into how the concepts of prostitution reflected conflicting and democratic political ideologies of the age.

Faraone and MCclure's text positions this enquiry on a three-tier structure that would come handy while discussing *Umrao Jan Ada*:

1. Social position of courtesans
2. Their legal status as it bore on marriage and taxation
3. The private laws that helped sustain it

This explains the hidden inertia associated with understanding the cult of the courtesans making it the most unspeakable profession of all times. This is because one needs to define the practice and demarcate the sexual and marital activities from one another. The extract from the novel *Umrao Jan Ada* will help us address the question of marriage for Umrao Jan:

> I have often heard people passing comments about those they call "prostitutes" or "courtesans." Most dismiss them out of hand, pointing out that in the place where they grew up they witnessed nothing but evil ways. They just followed the example of their mothers and sisters, who were in the same state. But daughters of respectable parents who leave

their home and follow the path of ruin deserve nothing more than to die in shame and denigration. I have already described my own background, and have nothing more to say except it was afterwards that I went astray. From this you may have the impression that I was mad for sex. You might think that my marriage was delayed, and I set my sights on some other man; when he left me, I passed on to another, but being unsuccessful with him, by degrees I made it my profession. That is very often the case, and I have seen and heard of many respectable women who have gone bad in this way. There are several reasons for it. One is that the girl attains puberty, but the parents do not arrange the marriage in time; another may be that their marriage does not work out well for them…. They might have suffered the awful blow of being widowed when they were still young. Losing patience, they found themselves in bad company. But in my case, it was a cruel stroke of fortune that led me into this miserable jungle, where there was no path other than that which led to ruin. (Ruswa, 7–8)

This passage is an extremely crucial insight to the entire discourse on marriage in the nineteenth century if placed along the Victorian sensibility. Umrao Jan Ada's conditioning within the kotha declines to look at the institution of marriage in a romantic manner. Her insights are governed by practicality and seem to be based on intelligence gathered from the society she lives in. This is why, in a way, we find it difficult to see Umrao herself becoming an outsider to the text and the time she lives in. The grandeur of the kotha culture seems to be a highly overwhelming and later on the nostalgic reflection on the cult being associated with low value and cheap pleasure is a hard-hitting fact. Her journey from honour to dishonour happens very quickly as the text opens at the brink of 1857. "She is lifted up for a moment into the spotlight by the story teller, but her place remains in the shadows of" (Faraone and MCclure, 60) the Mughal society. As Faraone and Laura K. MCclure rightly question the uncertainty, the term fictive transgression or transgressive fiction could be extended to Ruswa's authorial venture. Also, in the above extract one does find a sense of Socratic unity. This means that the individual is insignificant but the conversation between the two is revelatory of truth. Therefore, Ruswa becomes Umrao's mouth-piece with which the truth about the decadent phase of Lucknow. Umrao's monologue does inflict on the reader's the unknowability of the colonial design that neither opens up possibilities of her sustenance within tawaifdom nor create structures within society that can accommodate the Tradition. Therefore, Umrao's speech becomes an allegory to the colonial world. Her fragmentation is not because of a flaw in the cultural setting but is due to several disconnected things such as the replacement of Urdu with Hindi and English with the setting up of Fort William College, the colonizer's moralising tone and the tone of contempt for the class of courtesans and severe licensing of this art and shifting it under the wraps of a prostitution culture.

The concept of "free love" as discussed by Martha Feldman in *The Courtesan's Arts* was visibly strong in the Mughal era where the market morality and sexual contracts were the basic ingredients of the libidinal economy. The British probably found some "excess" and "lack" in the meaning of "love" and family life with respect to the emerging Victorian prudishness that definitely did not have an internal clarity of thoughts and led to a conflict between faith and doubt. Since the average Britisher suffered from the "moral gloom," the fact that the kotha-structure was institutionalized for entertaining the nawabs, fulfilling desires of men and imparting *adab* and *tehzeeb* to the sons of the elites made the exchange of this free love more functional and the Britishers even more uncomfortable with the native culture of India. Post the 1857 Mutiny, this concept of free love failed to carry itself into the changing society. Even the thought of learning Kathak and Hindustani Classical music post Independence was taken as a distasteful hobby to be taken up for the emergent middle class. Therefore, music and dance were the prime factors for the erotic capital brought in by the Mughal era. Let us juxtapose this against the Graeko-Roman culture. According to the Graeko-Roman culture, the *hetaira* is defined as the courtesan and the *porne* is the brothel worker.

> The term *Hetaira* is defined as the feminine form of *Hetairos* (the male friend), denoted a woman, usually celebrated, who was maintained by one man in exchange for his exclusive sexual access to her; typically she did not reside in his home. She participated in and embodied an economy of gift exchange that maintained, rather than severed, the connection between individuals. Alternately seductive and persuasive, providing her services in exchange for gifts, the *hetaera* perpetually often the possibility that she might refuse her favours. The *porne*, in contrast, belonged to the streets: she was the *hetaira's* nameless, faceless brothel counterpart and participated in a type of commodity exchange…" (MCclure, 7)

The woman's body is a site of struggle and being a courtesan problematizes it further. The figure of the courtesan is therefore, more prominently seen, watched and discussed socially, politically and legally post-1857. Umrao is childless like other courtesans. The kotha, in a way, becomes a strict place for eternal opposition between biological and aesthetic creativity. When compared to the Greek culture of courtesans, the Umrao-figure, in India,

27

seems like a valid school of thought existing since the pre-Mutiny Lucknow making her a highly self-conscious figure. If we probe a little further into history, the Indian chronological space also mentions the presence of Devdasis and Nartakis who excelled as women performers and nautch girls. However, they were temple dancers and were known to have specific features that classified them as temple goddesses. The existence of Umrao Jan Ada and the empowered kotha culture can be understood better in the light of Frances W. Pritchett's *Nets of Awareness* wherein she goes on to explain that the culture of Lucknow constituted itself on the fabric of the *mehfil*. The *mehfil* was formed by repetitive cultural associations and the more one repeats a particular gesture, the gesture becomes valuable. This shared code produces a kind of secular sociality which is one of the direct prerequisites of the musha'irah. Keeping Pritchett's idea in mind, Umrao can be seen as the culmination of such interpersonal relationships in the novel. As the novel foregrounds the musha'irah, Umrao Jan is brought into light. This was the entire social phenomena of the Age and not just a part of poetics. Urdu language and its poetic quality were about the strict rules of forming and reciting couplets.

> Musha'irahs are like professional workshops. As we have seen, a poet can be challenged by his peers for misusing a word, for slightly altering it, for unduly extending its associations, or for violating the logic of a traditional *mazmun*

> (like that of the wineglass as a "laughing" mouth), for these matters in which technical proficiency is involved. An ustad should be highly practiced and impeccable in his skills. His work must sustain—and even invite—comparison with that of the great masters of the past. (Pritchett, 77)

This gamut of extraordinariness forms the intellectual constitution of Umrao. Practicing a single pattern of song or poetry to its limit of exhaustion was the governing principle of the cult of the courtesan. Her instinct to be the best under the guidance of Khanum Jan and get trained in skills and Persian in no time makes her "gifted". And this can be the attribute of someone who is situated outside the social boundaries. Umrao Jan, in that case, becomes the outsider, the *bai*. Through Ruswa, this inversion becomes visible. The courtesan, if seen as the outsider, embodies the extraordinary, which is similar to creating a new marginal identity. If carefully looked into, this extraordinariness presents itself like the Unknown that Umrao Jan embodies and unfolds as the novel progresses. And this very journey from the Known to the Unknown energizes the plot of the novel. Sold for one hundred and fifty rupees, this kidnapping empowers Umrao in several ways. Kidnapping, therefore, becomes the moment when the protagonist is liberated from old contexts and put into new. This entire process weaves the theory of the margins deftly into the character. The courtesan becomes the woman in the margins but has her own center of gravity at the same time. This creates an interstice between two cognitive structures of two separate worlds. This forces one to think that the Hindu philosophy of the *mangal kavya* and bhakti poetry sung by *devdasi*s is no longer adequate to raise and answer questions of love, faith and doubt. This is what exactly empowers Umrao Jan Ada and the like.

The initial chapters in the novel foreground and establish the new domesticity of Umrao Jan Ada in Khanum's house. This mirrors and distorts the picture of the family from which she is plucked out. A new set of relationships envelop her as we see one family structure getting replaced by the other. This surrogate domesticity helps Umrao acquire a new name and a whole new set of skills combining the world of prostitution with the world of education. It is as if the kotha becomes synonymous with the modern-day finishing school. The following extract from the novel will give us an insight into the tedious and knowledge-based education that Umrao underwent:

> The maulvi taught me with great kindness. When we had finished the alphabet, we were introduced to the basic Persian language texts, such as the *Karima* and the *Mahmudnama*. Having learnt the *Ahmadnama* off by heart, we embarked upon Shaikh Saadi's *Gulistan*. The maulvi would teach two sentences and

make us commit them to memory. We were taught the meaning of each word, especially in the verses, and could repeat the constructions. Emphasis was put on reading and writing; our spelling was checked; and we were given letters to write. After mastering the *Gulistan*, other Persian texts were easy to me. It seemed that we had already done the lessons. We then studied Arabic grammar and a few books on logic. I sat at the maulvi's feet for about eight years. You know yourself how fascinated I was by poetry, and have no need to go into the details now. (Ruswa, 27)

Umrao during her rigorous training in Khanum's kotha was trained in *mujra* which is a hybrid form of the Indian dance form kathak and fusion of ghazal and thumri. These songs were sung to narrate the Krishna-Radha material relationship within the context of other *gopis*. Voicing the twinges of love and separation, these songs were a perfect fit for the mujra to operate. Umrao Jan Ada is therefore, within the Mughal domain that licenses such a cultural setup. She is categorically not someone like Bandit Queen or Mira Bai, who are the two most widely discussed transnational figures of the lower caste woman, an outlaw figure or a religious perpetrator. In *Humanities Underground: Taking on Mediocrity and Mechanization* (http://humanitiesunderground.wordpress.

com/category/performative/) a website portal discussing issues of literature and performativity critically says:

> But what if Umrao Jan tries to enter the realm of critical inquiry via an analytic of the British Empire in India in the nineteenth century? It is in the context of the 1857 series of wars between the British and the natives of India and the British repression of resistance against foreign rule that we need to understand the figure of Umrao. The British, in their imperial interests to rule India, annexed large territories of the princely states by dethroning the native kings of the region, often by claiming that they were inefficient rulers because their lives were spent in debauchery rampant in the Indian courts. Ray's *Satranj ki Khiladi* graphically demonstrates how tactically the British did engage in this game of chess with the Nawab of the Northeastern kingdom of Oudh and ousted him eventually. The British East India Company forcefully annexed Oudh by deposing its last independent ruler, Wajid Ali Shah, in 1856. This was one of the reasons that led to the outbreak of native resistance to British rule in 1857 in that part of the emerging nation.

During Umrao's course of learning we see Khanum Jan pointing out mistakes of the maulvi which shows Khanum's attention to details and her grounding in education. This was the kind of domesticity that Umrao would have probably lacked in all respects if she would not have been placed inside the kotha. How is this empowering? The gayaki transformation takes place between 1902 and 1912 in the recording studios of Calcutta and not with the British annexation of Awadh. What Umrao practised as a ritual in within the kotha found itself liberated in the recording studios. This is where the bai culture finds its first independence and thus, the empowerment to reach out to masses openly and at a larger scale. Apart from the that, Feldman and Gordon in "The Courtesan's Singing Body as Cultural Capital in Seventeenth-Century Italy" (*The Courtesan's Arts*) says that singing as an art was all the more problematic than speaking or discoursing in language. The "hurling of physical gestures" (189) along with the *harkat* in their songs giving out explicit expressions on love-pangs were the attributes of a courtesan. "Women who excelled in music-making were often assumed to be courtesans" (189).

> When the voice flowed out of the body it became something that could be exchanged, like the letters, books, and other currencies that courtesans circulated. It was a physical substance open for exchange that could

33

> increase a courtesan's sexual capital. (Gordon
> and Feldman, 194)

To shift our focus back to the Mughal era in India from the seventeenth century onwards, the people visiting the kothas were the sons of nawabs and nawabs themselves. These patrons had their favourite woman not solely on account of being in sexual relationships with her. There was a degree of friendship and courtship involved. For example, Umrao's relationship with Nawab Sultan was something close to romantic love. There was an element of reserve in the relationship which made it gracious and measured with decency. One certainly cannot call this a bawdy relationship, even though Nawab Sultan belongs to the aristocracy. Faiz Ali, Nawab Sultan's friend calls her sister-in-law with all due respect. Discussing the Shamsher Khan incident becomes necessary to bring out the conflicting interests in perception sustained by the kotha structure:

> "Khan Sahib! Are you going to use force?"
> "What do you mean "force"? This is a whore-house, isn't it?
>
> No one has a monopoly. And if I have to use force, I will. We'll see who can make me get up!"
> "Yes, there is a monopoly. It belongs to those who pay good money. No one else has the right to come."

"All right. I'll pay."

"No, it is not convenient now. Please come another time." (Ruswa, 61)

Two etiquettes come into conflict with this incident:

1. Shamsher Khan treats the kotha as a common street kotha where *randi*s are available to all customers.
2. Nawab Sultan treats kotha as upper class elite does and respects the decorum that is attached to it.

Shamsher Khan's point of view shows the beginning of threat to the kotha structure. This indicates that the cult of the courtesan, their aura and respectability could be dented very easily. In another incidence, when Umrao Jan visits Faizabad during one of her performance, she is threatened by her brother that in case she does not leave the village, she will be killed. In this case, the empowered courtesan is put to test. How empowered is she after all? The respectability of the tawaif is almost always under a siege bringing out the vulnerability of the status. This duality in the kotha structure is discriminating as it allows the patriarchy to participate and also resist it side by side. Dis-empowerment runs as the undercurrent in this post-Mutiny novel. In comparison to this, women who followed the conventional norms of domesticity were outside the purview of the cardinal sin. The domestic woman was to function within the realm of prescriptive texts such as *Bihishti Zevar* (1905) that was published in the twentieth century. It was meant to guide women on leading a normal course of a happy married life. Thanawi justified the need for this book by stating,

> the world they lived in was seriously awry, and they set out to reform it through the methods they held most central, namely, education of religious leaders, preaching and teaching and public debate…. The *Bihishti Zewar* was intended to provide basic education for a respectable Muslim woman. It rapidly became a classic gift for Muslim brides, who "entered their husband's home with the Holy Qur'an in one hand and the *Bihishti Zewar* in the other. (Thanawi, Note on Translation, 2)

Within the domestic sphere, women were treated as subordinates of men who needed the guidance of people like Thanawi who could guide them for a superior living. The laws of marriage also denied women their share of inheritance or the *Mahr.* There were many such strict code of conduct that were meant to "enhance a girl's domestic role" (Thanawi, 26). Comparing women confined within marriage and the life of courtesans, the limits of a prosperous existence seem far more liberating in case of the latter.

So does this make the culture breathe its last and face denigration even today? Even though the distinction between proficient courtesans and randis and domnis existed, what made the categorization collapse into one making them into a common term—prostitute—a name by which we know them today. The courtesan figure is now perceived as vulgar, low, evil, degraded, a cheap source of entertainment or homeless women, in general, who are sexually promiscuous.

The Presence of the Courtesan within the Arrangement of the Musha'irah

The magical spirit of the musha'irah has been known to cast a spell on the minds of the listeners. *Umrao Jan Ada* too starts with a musha'irah which Munshi Ahmad Hussain and Ruswa himself recite. Not being able to accept an "absent praise" (Ruswa, 16) coming from the next room where a courtesan resided in isolation, Ruswa convinced her to join them for a couplet or two. The conversation gives us an insight into the politically and artistically charged lifestyle of the Mughal kingdom in Lucknow. A musha'irah according to Faratullah Baig in *The Last Musha'irah of Dehli* calls is:

> a poetic symposium, soiree at which poets of the day read their original works for pleasure. A musha'irah is not an easy form of entertainment. It demands full intellectual

and emotional participation within the prescribed framework of aesthetic conventions set by the masters long ago. In course of time musha'irahs became, in addition, excellent forums for literary criticism, disputation and, sometimes, on-the-spot poetic compositions. But the main purpose of a musha'irah is to offer opportunities for the enjoyment of reciting and listening to selected ghazal poetry. (Baig, 28)

In the above extract, the phrase "intellectual and emotional participation" becomes self-explanatory as it gives us the agency to distinguish between familial marriages and compassionate marriages. The performative aspect in the life of a courtesan emphasizes more on performativity involved in leading the courtesan way of life. Tawaifdom encouraged a ceremonious celebration of art that was presented according to customs of the day. The Mughal society licensed such cultural expressions that were denied in severe aspects for the domesticated woman. The tawaifdom does give the patriarch a scope for a compassionate "marriage" or a "union" of ideas, whereas, women who are not courtesans fail to offer this possibility, that in turn, justifies the smooth presence of kothas during the Mughal reign.

Moving into the setting of the musha'irah, the *baithak* usually consisted of poets and ghazal singers who started the recitation of poetry and couplets.

It is held at the aristocratic hour between nine and ten at night after dinner and goes on till dawn with a feast of ghazal after ghazal... Needless to say no women were present at the old traditional musha'irahs. But since women were the object of longing and despair in much of the later ghazal poetry, their absence made them all the more desired and intriguing. The presiding or the host poet was assigned the central seat in a more or less circular seating arrangement. In front of him was placed the shama', symbol of the poetic muse. The shama' was passed on to the poet whose turn it was to present his ghazal. (Baig, 31—32)

Traditional musha'irahs did not regulate the direct presence of the female. Women may have had zenana musha'irahs. In certain cases, the princesses or the wealthy aristocrats present in the king's harem or the concubines present in the harems would have had their *kalaam* to be recited. The notion of women writing poetry was acceptable but it was behind the scenes of patriarchal society. However, with Ruswa we do see the woman voicing poetry with full power and élan that communicate to us the visibly changing history of Lucknow. The desire for a woman within a traditional setting of the musha'irah that was kept intact in a male gathering now gets transformed into the physical presence of the woman herself. This also puts forth the performative aspect making the male desire the courtesan more vividly within the kotha structure. However, the possible explanation can be that, whereas the musha'irah only catered to the poetic quality, knowledge and charm of the poet, the musha'irah within the geometrically fortified interiors of the kotha gains a more performative and erotic aspect.

The position of the courtesan within the musha'irah is indicative of limitless consumerist desire present in the changing phase of Lucknow. "It is the tawa'if's unencumbered identity as a woman that enabled the courtesan to produce a sensual gendered cultural experience for her male patrons in return for the rewards they offer" (Feldman and Gordon, 322). In this case, the identity of womanhood has been able to ascribe itself in the kotha structure and a social branding of the courtesans created to mark their degree of distinction in their profession is also visible. (This will be discussed later in the chapter in opposition to an altered form of branding introduced by the Britishers post Mutiny to segregate prostitution as a different layer of society carrying venereal diseases). In contrast to the domesticated woman, the prosperous courtesan was supposed to be the master of gestures, Persian studies, fine clothes and jewelleries, dance and music and well-versed the art of retaining her patron for as long as possible. A renowned courtesan's price in the market would be at a higher end as she would have been more in demand. The khangis or the lower ranking prostitutes were in their profession in a more direct way and maintained the hierarchy of being lowest in the ring. The brand value and their power helped not only demarcate the living spaces within the kotha structure but also channelized a way of giving authorizations to relationships with men at their disposal. Umrao always had the liberty to choose her patrons and the *chaudharayan* ensured that Umrao entertained only one patron at a time.

Placing Umrao Jan Ada within the Courtesan Classification and Highlighting the Sexual Politics of the Age (1800 onward)

Courtesanship and its sexual politics need to be reconsidered in this light from 1800 onward. The positioning of courtesans becomes important in India when studied in context of British colonization and their offence towards the nautch and other practices such as the practice of Sati in India. This was the first phase of feminism that can be chronicled in India's history. The second phase can be traced 1915 onward till the Quit India Movement and the third phase is the post-independence phase of feminism. The feminist question in the context of tawaifdom remains pertinent as this profession cannot be ascribed to a mainstream feminist movement as such. Similar movements till date talk more about alternative sexualities but not alternative modes of existence and agency available to women.

> [W]hy didn't the women's movements in India consider sex workers as an integral part of the women's movements. Why are sex worker's movements limited and isolated to sex workers only? Is prostitution perhaps too alien to mainstream and particularly middle-class sexual experiences, which is the basis for mainstream movement? If the sex workers' movement is to have a voice, where is to be placed in the context of feminist discourse? Even within sex workers' movements, and the organizations involved with them, there are contrasting views and ideologies. Is this internal rift of opinions further mention its interaction with mainstream movements? (Sahni, 15–16)

The courtesan culture stands degraded right from the post-Mutiny phase because with the coming of the Britishers and their leaving the country, the process of urbanization had already started restructuring itself. With the *devdasi*s and the *tawaif*s prostitution was more ritualized following a certain code of conduct within temples or within kothas. Soon after, it was solely based on a monetary exchange during the transitional phase of Lucknow 1850 onward. The hierarchy is as follows:

1. tawaifs and deredar tawaifs
2. zanan khangis

3. zanan bazaris
4. kasbis
5. takabis
6. domnis, kasbis or takabis

The tawaifs and the deredar tawaifs (camping courtesans) were known to be highly accomplished in the skills of singing and dancing and hailed from the court of Shuja-ud-Daula. Veena Talwar Oldenburg, in her works, combines these two categories into one which does not take away their individual qualities. These tawaifs boasted of refined manners, etiquettes, knowledge of cultural books, music, and literature. They excelled in poetry and *qasida*s. They traded their skills on the basis of patronage and the gifts they received. The nawabs who visited them also belonged to the elite class and had a finely honed taste for poetry and camaraderie. Therefore, sexual relationship was only a part of this cult. Strict codes of conduct were followed and maintained inside the kothas of the tawaifs and the patrons who stayed back for the night paid heavy sums of money to these courtesans. The rest left after the mujra session ended. These tawaifs had tremendous power attached to them as they stayed on with the elites and other wealth-emerging sectors of the time. Many nawabs sent their sons to the tawaifs for high education, etiquette, and social values. In case of Umrao Jan Ada, both Nawab Sultan and Faiz Ali shower gifts at her and desire her company. However, in this case, Umrao breaks the code of conduct by meeting

Nawab Sultan in secrecy and later on running away with Faiz Ali who is a dacoit. As for, Gauhar Mirza, who is her first lover, she "unofficially" has her first sexual encounter with him against the will and knowledge of Khanum Jan. Her desires and the will to break-free from the luxuries of kotha also resurrects her empowered self that she finds during her temporary passion for Gauhar Mirza. It is only with Nawab Sultan and later Faiz Ali that she emerges as a much more self-aware character who is capable of making her own choices. This is a definite pointer to the empowerment of the courtesan figure.

We also see Umrao performing in the court of Wajid Ali Shah. And this is when she decides to return to Khanum Jan's kotha. Umrao is shown to be changing due to the changes brought in by the men in her life. This makes her as a disempowered woman. Musharraf Ali Farooqi's *Beyond Clay and Dust*, the main character Gohar Jan dies an insignificant death and she is denied a common burial ground in the end. It becomes necessary to deconstruct Umrao's history and scrutinize, in this process, the other histories that are created—a part of which prostitution is, today. It can be asserted that Umrao is still in the process of "becoming" and Ruswa is framing her thoughts. Her existence is literature in itself. She comes alive through Ruswa and sustains herself through her knowledge of literature. Within the text, we see a kind of self-fashioning that Umrao undertakes to make her better than the existing courtesans and to get noticed. Umrao at multiple points in the novel seems to be in full control of her story and insights such as "If I had not acquired this taste for reading, I would not have been able to live very long" show that her knowledge, strenuous education and skills acquired in the kotha made her strong. This indeed makes Umrao a timeless, culture-less[10] universal existence in the end as one certainly doubts as to how much of courtesanship is she able to retain in herself. This self-awareness present in her distances her from her own profession. Thus, we see a dual existence by the end of the novel:

With Umrao's prosperity: The audience is the mute spectator

With Umrao's loss: It becomes a shared silence that is kept under wraps by the moral uprightness of the patriarchy.

Within the domain of tawaifdom, discussing the zanan khangis and zanan bazaris is also relevant. Zanan Khangis or the household women were very Lucknow-specific. Due to the 1856–57 revolt, many domestic women switched to the profession of being tawaifs due to poverty. However, these women indulged in sexual activities without the knowledge or consent of their family members and did it silently. This is an extremely different practice of prostitution seen in Lucknow. This muted presence began then, and has seeped into the seams of society now. This category did not take into account

---

[10] Culture-less signifies an existence that raises the Spectacle above cultural differences and restrictions.

music, art or literature but a pure bodily transaction and set in motion *randi bazi*. The fee was fixed and one could not bargain with them. *Ada* and *adab* went missing from the scene drastically. Many *khangi*s were known to keep *dalal*s for fixing up with clients. Unlike the tawaifs who traded within the kotha, the khangis traded on the streets and by-lanes. This change is significant as *adab* did not take much time to get replaced by *ayyashi*. Culture, as a result, faced the dent of non-uniformity that made the cult of the courtesan suffer the burden of the changing times. Those who were once assets and up keepers of culture began to be deemed a disgrace for the culture after society faced violent ruptures. An approach that defines the cult of the courtesan not only in terms of agency but also a system that had an internal structure that was self-sustaining on the basis of arts and culture (which were the symbols of the Mughal Age in India) should be in progress. New and meaningful ways of understanding the courtesan way of life with their remarkable taste in music and dance should be a part of the cultural study and its validation. This will help in freeing cult of the courtesan from a gamut of double-edged meanings and negative associations.

Works Cited

"Off Modern: A Conversation with Raqs." Web. 30 May 2012 <http://humanitiesunderground.wordpress.com/category/performative/>.

Baig, Mirza Farhatullah. The Last Mushaira of Dehli. Trans. Akhtar Qamber. New Delhi: Orient Blackswan, 2010.

Chattopadhyay, Bankimchandra. *The Poison Tree*. Trans. Marian Maddern and S. N. Mukherjee. Delhi: Penguin, 1996.

Dewey, Susan. *Hollow Bodies: Institutional Responses to Sex Trafficking in Armenia*, Bosnia and India. Virginia: Kumarian, 2008.

Eraly, Abraham. *The Mughal World*. Delhi: Eastern Book Corporation, 2007.

Faraone, Christopher A., and Laura K. McClure, ed. *Prostitutes and Courtesans in the Ancient World the University of Wisconsin Press*. Wisconsin: Monroe Street Madison, 2006.

Farooqi, Musharaff Ali. *Between Clay and Dust*. Trans. David Davidar. New Delhi: Aleph Book Company, 2012.

Feldman, Martha and Bonnie Gordon. *The Courtesan's Arts: Cross-cultural Perspectives*. USA: Oxford University Press, 2006.

http://en.wikipedia.org/wiki/Plutocracy PLUTOCRACY

Lal, K. S. *The Mughal Harem*. New Delhi: Aditya Prakashan, 1992.

Lal, Vinay. "The Courtesan and the Indian Novel." *Indian Literature* 139 (Sep.–Oct. 1995): 164–70.

Maulana Ashraf Ali Thanvi. Introduction. *Bihishti Zewar* (Special Edition). India: DK Publishers Illustration and OUP Publication, 2003, p. 775.

Illustrated Oxford English Dictionary. India: DK Publishers Illustration and OUP Publication, 2003.

Pritchett, Frances W. *Nets of Awareness: Urdu Poetry and its Critics*. California: University of California Press, 1994.

Ruswa, Mirza Mohammad Hadi. *Umrao Jan Ada: Courtesan of Lucknow*. Trans. David Matthews. New Delhi: Rupa & Co., 2007.

Sahni, Rohini. *Prostitution and Beyond: An Analysis of Sex Workers in India*. New Delhi: SAGE, 2008.

Tharu, Susie and K. Lalita, ed. *Women Writing in India: 600 BC to the Present, Volume 1.* Delhi: Oxford University Press, 1991.

CHAPTER TWO

BEGUM SAMRU: A SUITABLE COUNTERPART?

In the study of the art of courtesans and the culture that sustained them, Begum Samru could become an interesting historical case study. The Begum started her life as a nautch girl and went on to become a noted political figure of the Mughal Era. Whether Begum Samru can be regarded as an appropriate counterpart of Umrao Jan Adas in the times will be glanced at during the course of the study. The pre-Mutiny Lucknow was already witnessing the European anxiety about the way of life which included issues of the notion of the "family," race, caste, color, and sexuality. Broadly speaking, three types of family models can be seen during pre-Mutiny Lucknow:

the conventional domestic family bound by marriage, the family within the kotha where the *chaudharayan* is the matrilinear head taking care of and managing the courtesans working under her, and the European family model where the British men kept Indian concubines, had children with them but did not marry them and left them some fortune after their death. Consequently, all afore mentioned models of the family were under scrutiny. Begum Samru would fall under the third model of the family-structure. She is a historical character who presents the example of the extent of agency available to women through the cult of the courtesan.

A crucial element while discussing the anxieties of courtesan culture is the question of its destabilization during the Mutiny. The heterogeneous Mughal culture seemingly had more tolerance towards the largely homogenous British society than vice versa. And this is why Begum Samru becomes a typical point of introspection- a nautch girl who underwent baptism to turn catholic and remained Walter Reinhardt's concubine till his death. She was one of the most influential women of her time, and had close contacts with the British regime. Begum Samru's repute derives from a self-confidence, style and élan that could be regarded as a legacy of her past. A courtesan making a difference to the political atmosphere and maintaining regiments of soldiers for state protection highlights her potential as a knowledgeable woman who was well acquainted with the intricacies and politics of the Mughal culture in India.

Her life, as documented by Nicholas Shreeve in *Dark legacy: The Fortunes of Begum Samru* seems politically influential and represents an extremely desexualized life, directing the libidinal urges into the domain of the political, which makes her an institution in herself. In the book, Begum Samru's autobiography is discussed scantily in terms of her beauty and more in relation to her aptitude and her affinity towards political prowess. Beauty brings in the problems of description. Typical to several accounts of courtesan culture compiled and described in *The Courtesan's Arts* that covers the courtesan culture of Greece, Rome, Italy, China, India and Japan, the courtesan way of life is described heavily in terms of the dresses and the knowledge of selecting the right kimono for the right season and the jewelleries that are to be worn as adornments apart from the elaborate head gears chosen by courtesans for their evening performances. These descriptions make the life of a courtesan not a sexual one but an erotic one. Begum Samru's description on the other hand, is represented in a completely desexualized manner wherein her dressing-up is not given much space. Therefore, in this case, we see the first rejection of this "necessary supplement" of adorning the body. Shreeve's book on Begum Samru locates the position of women beyond the fetish-syndrome and study the courtesan-politician model sans a moral debate. However, one is not sure that this avoidance of problematization is necessarily a fruitful one.

Paralleling Umrao's life that journeys from the naive Ameeran to the artful courtesan Umrao Jan Ada, Begum Samru changed her name too. Earlier known as Farzana Zeb un-Nissa, Begum Samru came to be known as Begum Joanna Nobilis Sombre. This is indicative of the expanse of culture she embodied within herself and her political affiliations that spread far and wide. This change of name seems to have "modified their cultural practices (of being a courtesan) as a way of negotiating greater advantages for her successes in political and military matters" (Chakravarty, 147–48). This also can be treated as an act of "reconfiguring identity" (Chakravarty, 148) questioning the identity of the woman not only from a racial point of view but also acknowledging a fight for a statistical survival in the books of the British. At this point in time, Durba Ghosh's attempt at understanding the reason for taking on different names comes in handy:

> The kinds of conventions used in recording the names of people who were born, who died or were married within the East India Company's dominions confirms that colonial subjects were recorded in colonial archives only when necessary to mark out racial and social status... (Ghosh, 19)

Being the "wife" of Walter Reinhardt, was this the reason for her baptism? Would she have prospered more if she would have retained her Mughal identity? Being politically aware and exposed to Reinhardt's career graph, she must have known about the political changes introduced to redistribute wealth, land and political power, which were being practiced by the British as a part of colonial political documentation. Right after the Mutiny of 1857, several women, soldiers and common Indian servants of the Britishers were converted to Christianity. These converted people consisted of both Muslims and Hindus. Ghosh observes that "while keeping a native female companion and living like a native was a sign of cosmopolitanism, or broad-mindedness, of a level of sophistication that was unavailable to those who were at 'home', it was also a sign of the kind of cultural and racial hybridity that threatened the social whiteness of colonial societies" (36). Therefore, the substantiation of Begum Samru and Walter Reinhardt's love for each other is a lesser possibility. This explains the concept of "reconfiguring identity" as one model of explanation. This approach exteriorizes the process of undergoing baptism or taking on of another name that takes place outside the walls of the kotha which is within the domain of the political. Another model of interpreting the process of courtesans undergoing this reconfigured identity can be seen and understood within the premises of the kotha structure. Veena Talwar Oldenburg in the essay 'The Case of the Courtesans of Lucknow' tells us about a young Persian scholar who is born within the kotha and is called Chote Miyan and is never given a proper name. Oldenburg writes:

He explained why he had only been given a pet name [roughly, Mr Small] instead of a serious Muslim family name. He was the son of a courtesan and she had never revealed to him the identity of his father. Ironically, his sad life story had all the elements of the socialization and upbringing accorded to a girl in a "normal" household.

While I love and respect my mother and all my "aunts" [other courtesans] and my grandmother, my misfortune is that I was born a son and not a daughter in their house. When a boy is born in the kotha, the day is without moment, even one of quiet sadness. When my sister was born there was a joyous celebration that was unforgettable. Everyone received new clothes, there was singing, dancing, and feasting. My aunts went from door to door distributing sweets. My sister is, today, a beautiful, educated, propertied woman. She will also inherit what my mother and grandmother own. She will have a large income from rents... I am educated, but I have no money or property. Jobs are very hard to come by, so I live in a room and subsist on a small allowance that my mother gives in exchange for running errands for her and helping her deal with her lawyers. [She was trying to evict a tenant from a house she

> owned.] She paid for my education but a
> degree is pretty worthless these days. My only
> hope is that I may marry a good woman who
> has money and who gives me sons so they can
> look after me in my old age... Otherwise my
> chances in life are pretty dim. Funny isn't it,
> how these women have made life so topsy-
> turvy? (Oldenburg, 261–62)

This reveals to us the absolute inverted nature of gender structure that operated within the kotha structure. While the courtesan enjoyed titles such as *bai* and *Jan,* the male was depicted as the non-functional and purposeless gender than the female. This kind of identity of a woman born inside the kotha marks the personality of a woman as the stronger sex. She undergoes an elaborate naming ceremony while the male assumes passivity even while he is named. Anybody can be called a Chote Miyan. We know of only one Umrao Jan Ada. A female's identity within the kotha and her renaming becomes a distinct principle of the reconfiguration of identity that marks her professional courtesan status. In the traditional Mughal society in India, "respectable" women who were rich and belonged to the propertied class also carried suffixes such as Begum that were traditionally added to their names. This prevented them from entering the direct male sexualized gaze that could be freely done within the confines of the kotha. The title Begum helped women negotiate their social positions and gained recognition with respect to becoming legal heirs to properties, wills, letters and political debates. Thus, the figure of courtesan and her way of life created cultural polar identities- the powerless man, the domestic woman and the courtesan.

Lucknow was passing through an unstable political environment due to British intervention in the late nineteenth and early twentieth century and keeping native concubines had become the trend among the Britishers. The dates of Begum Samru are only tentative, they could probably be around 1751–1836. As stated in Gautam Chakravarty's *The Indian Mutiny and the British Imagination,* Begum Samru's career graph is exceptional. Her success in political and military matters outdid her capacity as a dancing girl and she went on to become a landholder in Northern India. Even though there are conflicting reports that trace her birth as a Kashmiri descendant or being born to the second wife of a nobleman in Kutana, the culture that made this possible and conditioned her was the rough and strenuous schooling that the courtesans had to undergo before they were launched as professional performers in front of select audience. According to Brajendranath Banerji's *Begum Samru,* J. Baillie Fraser's *Military Memoirs of Lt. Col. James Skinner* and Thomas Bacon's *First Impression and Studies from Nature in Hindoostan,* her birth has some conflicting reports:

> According to some sources, she was born to the second wife of a nobleman in Kutana, a

village in Meerut district, near Delhi. Other sources claimed she was of Kashmiri descent. All of these sources date from the period *after* her ascent to the position of landholder of Sardhana and seek to validate her elevation from a dancing girl to a woman of noble stature. She did not leave any autobiographical accounts and aside from her letters to Mughal and British officials in which she attempted to extract political concessions, her life as she might have narrated it is absent from historical scrutiny. (Chakravarty, 149)

She began her career as a nautch girl and went on to become Walter Reinhardt's close companion filling in the void of his first wife who was mentally unstable. In this regard, Warren Hastings' comment needs menion:

The naturally quick understanding of his (Sombre's) wife had been strengthened and expanded by the education which he had given her the means of attaining and she became a most active and judicious assistant to him in all his most intricate concerns. She took the field with him, and in action was borne in her palanquin from rank to rank, encouraging the men who were enchanted with her heroism. (Shreeve, 51)

As researched and documented by Nicholas Shreeve, in one of the letters written by Major Polier (a Swiss engineer officer in the Company) around the 1770s, Walter Reinhardt did not know how to read and write "who was much afraid of the English... wears a Mogul dress and has a zenana."[11] Shreeve clarifies that this report was "full of contradictions and raises plenty of questions" (66). In this case, if Begum Samru had risen from the ranks of Reinhardt's zenana, this adds to her desexualization further through her extensive knowledge in education, arts and literature along with the politics of the time. One can easily ascribe Begum Samru's affinity for court politics and not bawdy politics. Her knowledge about court mechanisms alone sustained her, even after Reinhardt's death as she went on to increase her property and the army of soldiers. Her terms with the British government are evidence of her judicious networking skills. Probably, her education within the kotha structure helped her negotiate the financial provisions of the Mughal age. According to Nicholas Shreeve, Reinhardt's political career realized its full potential only towards

---

[11] "The literal meaning of Zenana is "of the women" or "pertaining to women". It contextually refers to the part of a house belonging to a Muslim family in South Asia reserved for the women of the household. The Zenana are the inner apartments of a house in which the women of the family live" (<http://en.wikipedia.org/wiki/Zenan> last visited on 28 May 2012).

the end of his life as the Britishers never trusted him for his turncoat nature towards politics. And this is when Begum Samru moves toward gaining complete power over the army post Reinhardt's death. In the first few years of her career she was popularly known as "The Widow of Samru" which indicates her affiliation to what was achieved by Reinhardt. From her identity of being inseparable from Reinhardt's political achievements, historians find her growing and changing into "Begum Samru," defying her identity as merely someone's widow.

In addition to being successful politically, she was also famous for the lavish nautch parties she threw for her European guests. Drawing immediate parallels of her taste for nautch parties with her origin is not the only focus here as the cultural significance of the existence of kothas and harems needs to be justified in this context. The harem, or the *zenana*, was a significant local place for cultural negotiations. In the *Lady's Diary of the Seige of Lucknow* and other similar British accounts on the Indian culture, the harem was supposed to be a secluded place where the women were confined for pleasure. On the other hand, Persian accounts that describe the purpose of harems within the eighteenth century politics state,

> the harem was central to negotiating family
> and dynastic politics. The women's quarters
> of the local courts were important spaces for
> exchanging information, hearing gossip, and
> conducting negotiations. The women of the

zenana, most often the wives, mothers, and
daughters of local rulers often contributed a
great deal to the running of the household as
well as the imperial realm. (Ghosh, 75)

Samru stayed with Walter Reinhardt throughout
his career in Farzana till Reinhardt's death. Her rise
in political stature foregrounds the already politically-
inclined behaviour of the kotha women. Begum Samru
might have practice the art of tawaifdom in Delhi and
Reinhardt's visit to India[12] around the second half of 1700s
must have exposed him to the culture of the courtesans
and tawaifs. M. N. Sharma, in his book *The Life and
Times of Begum Samru of Sardhana* mentions briefly:

At this point in time, according to some
accounts, he reportedly changed his name
to Sommers or Summers which was later
corrupted into Samru by his Indian underlings.
Other accounts suggest that Samru was
derived from Sombre, the appellation given
by his soldiers to describe a man who was
dark in skin as well as personality.... She
became Samru ki Begum or Samru's Begum.
(Chakravarty, 150)

---

[12] He started as a mercenary soldier with the French army
and in 1756 he changed sides and joined the East India
Company.

The title Begum was attached to women from noble descent and by retaining the title Begum and attaching Reinhardt's name along with it; she defined and stamped her attachment with him forever. Eighteenth century India had defined *bibi/begum* as the wife or the lady companion of an Englishman. The *burra bibi* was the Englishwoman (the wife of the Englishman). "This term came to have a pejorative tinge attached to it, particularly after the middle of the nineteenth century" (Ghosh, 33). Begum Samru's influential politics and her career as the ruler of Sardhana with the weight of the title Begum is a matter worth contemplating. Her initial conditioning within the kotha and becoming Reinhardt's companion only to get more exposed into the political situations of the state would not have happened if she would have been within a "legitimate" marital circumstance. Begum Samru "did two things simultaneously: one was to affirm herself as a noblewoman, the second was to solidify her connection to Samru, who was by the late 1760s a formidable officer who commanded four battalions and about 2,000 soldiers" (Chakravarty, 151). Similar to Begum Samru and Walter Reinhardt, James Kirkpatrick and his begum were another colonial family. James Kirkpatrick was high-ranking official in the East India Company's army who married a local native called Khair-un-nissa that further stirred in the British insecurities on the interracial marriages that could possibly "corrupt" the White racial purity of the Company in India. Historical accounts tell us that James too, built a home for Khair-un-Nissa and himself that was part imperial and part Islamic in its construction and had a kotha inside the house. However, the level of state-interference in their marriage was much higher here than in the relationship of Begum Samru and Walter Reinhardt. Begum Samru's retention of her title and Khair-un-Nissa's dismissal of it (no where it is mentioned that she carried this title with her) brings out the stronger personality trait present in the former. However, the concern for racial impurities, class status, social opportunities were at its peak in 1800 when Kirkpatrick met Khair-un-Nissa. Begum Samru by being the "Begum" undermined British superiority in many respects. In the process, she emerged as a strong cultural character by extending the same characteristics she acquired as a nautch girl.

Begum Samru, therefore, can be viewed as an extension of Umrao Jan Ada. It is as if Umrao Jan Ada is the text and Begum Samru, the *Ur*-text[13]—this Umrao-Begum Samru dichotomy will span the degeneration of Lucknow in its entirety as it would reflect the way these courtesans positioned themselves and their identities. Had Umrao Jan been given a chance to grow politically, then a figure like Begum Samru would have been the most rational extension of her. As is mentioned in Martha

---

[13] In German language, 'Ur' means original. If we treat *Umrao Jan Ada* as a historical fictional document of Awadh, then Begum Samru becomes the original case in history required to supplement Ruswa's case.

Feldman and Bonnie Gordon's edited book *Courtesan's Arts: Cross Cultural Perspectives*:

> In part this is because even for those who live with them the courtesans have been hard to know. They are fundamentally elusive fantasies of the imagination. Yet it is precisely this seductive vagueness, this endless deferral as Davidson describes it, that has made the courtesan so enticing to her consumers and critics that keeps even those who vanished thousands of years ago still entangling us in their bright web. (Feldman and Gordon, 5)

In the above extract, words used to define the courtesan way of life are as follows: "hard to know," "elusive fantasies," part of "imagination," "seductive vagueness," the art of "endless deferral," and "enticing." These words can be seen as pejorative on one hand, yet on the other, they seem to infuse great power in the figure of the courtesan. The ambiguity attached to a courtesan's love affairs serves to provide a very reductive view of the entire institution of the kotha. A characteristic trait of the kotha is that it becomes the site of exchanges that allows the exchange of time, exchange of body, conversation and exchange of gifts and money. This mode of payment for allowing such exchanges to take place need not necessarily be financial. Poems, *nazm*s and ghazals also formed a part of giving "gifts" to the courtesans that brings into focus a dynamic power play which is not only related to sexual power play within the kotha.

If one were to examine the nature of the power and position of the King (in general), his power is generally reliant on external power such as force, military power, secularity, sacredness, just and as an object of adoration. On the other hand, the woman's power (can be a begum, a courtesan or a domesticated woman) comes not from any kind of secular power or external force but comes from the power of her chastity. The nature of this power of being chaste is sacred which can tread the course of the Divine. This power in itself derives from something which is inherent in women, that is, their sexuality. And therefore, the power of such chastity is defined in terms of self-restraint that tawaifdom does not encourage. The flourishing of "free love" and unrestrained glances on patrons enhance the erotic aspect of the courtesan making her an object that has the potential to be unchaste. Also, it must be noted that forcing someone to be chaste does not make one chaste because sexual intentions do foreground sooner or later. Therefore, marriage becomes the ultimate solution-model or a remedy-model for curbing sexual display. On the other hand, female sexuality is something that is perceived as a threat. And this is why the way of life of the tawaif is supposed to be hard-hearted and impenetrable, which can be a potentially destructive and harmful arrangement (according to patriarchal interpretations). In the entire idea of valourization of chastity, a prior "fear" of transgression from chastity to unchastity and from fidelity to infidelity within the feminine realm is required for the woman to become conscious of the patriarchal existence and fear an industry that is so proficient in arts.

In case of *Umrao Jan Ada*, the readers never really get to know whom she totally loved. Therefore, her first sexual encounter also with Gauhar Mirza does not take her chastity away from her. Therefore, with Begum Samru and Umrao Jan Ada, the economy[14] of the female comes into play. Post annexation of Awadh, "prostitution" in Lucknow is no more legitimate. Control and licensing of prostitution moves from the feudal network of patronage to a more bureaucratic network of patronage where there is a lot more regulation followed and maintained. *Umrao Jan Ada* also begins with the violation of the Space of the courtesan. In this transfer of power from nawabi Lucknow to British Lucknow, the shift of control that affects this Space becomes crucial for a discussion. The plutocracy of the Mughal reign could not continue to command respect from the courtesan culture, especially once the concept of the hygiene became a general symbol for public health, according to British interpretations. (This will be discussed in detail in chapter three.) In European history, the general tendency and the inclination to attain power have been imagined as a man's domain, and women seem to have occupied more of an ambivalent position in the hierarchy of power. As Lynn Hunt insightfully says, "the

---

[14] Women treated as goods and commodities.

social and political order cannot be reproduced without women, but women were almost always imagined as dangerous if they meddled in public – that is – political concerns" (Hunt, 2).

Talking about the political career of Walter Reinhardt in India, we see that he is a German butcher's son. Reinhardt had already gained some tax-free property in Northern India as a reward for his meritorious service in the army. This piece of land generated good income for Reinhardt in India.

> According to several sources, Begum Samru had been central in the behind-the-scenes negotiations at the Mughal court in securing the *jaidad* for Samru in Sardhana. The decision to settle in Sardhana, the region in which she was born, was the Begum's choice. Before Samru's death, the Begum had lived among the troops and had formed strong bonds with the officers in Samru's battalions. Thus, when Samru died, she apparently became the popular choice among Samru's officers to be his successor, superseding the claims of Samru's son by another woman. Begum Samru was favoured by the Mughal emperor and soon after Samru's death, she was granted the lands that were previously granted to Samru. Thereafter, she became known as Begum Samru of Sardhana and

> in addition to being a landed magnate, she
> also became commander of four battalions.
> (Chakravarty, 154)

Reinhardt's acquisition of power and Begum Samru's expansion and spreading of the power structures in Northern India and with the British gives us an idea about her power to network. This kind of networking might have started off along with her obscure origins during her brief career as a nautch girl and can provide a clue to her political competency. In the context, Marie Antoinette (1755–1793) becomes a good contrast example for our reference. During the 1780s, Marie Antoinette, the former queen of France, was known for debauchery and pornographic pamphlets that were circulated questioning her sexual promiscuity that declared one of the darkest periods of France in terms of understanding the "perils" of female sexuality. The rumours were that she had committed incest with her eight-year old post which the entire Women's Political Clubs in France were shut down. Without going further into the crevices of the political situations of France, the body of a woman, irrespective of her being the ruler or a commoner, is always weighed equally in terms of sex and the social class they represent. Marie Antoinette was the negative point of reference for France then onwards and still is, in the pages of history. Similarly, tawaifdom becomes the negative point of reference for Mughal studies where the culture is shown to be in an irreparable state of "excesses" and "ridden with incest and lust." Such social tensions get more space once it cowers on the borders of incest and prostitution. It should be made clear that Marie Antoinette, in this discussion, is taken as an example that draws a trans-national and a patriarchal response to the social turmoil caused by her that put an entire nation into questioning and self-questioning. A similar response is generated in several European accounts about the private lives of Mughals in India who were "sexually active" and maintained multiple wives for leisure. If not in the social space, then in art and literature, the woman's body continues to suffer from the male's objective representation of women. In such a scenario, Begum Samru is one of the distinguished women politicians who introduce the concept of "politico-economy" within the capacity of the kotha from the perspective of running a battalion and a state without bringing into play her sexual identity or "body" politics. Leading four battalions Begum Samru's strong connections with the Mughal court is evident from the fact that she never lets go off the prefix Begum from her name.

The power politics of Awadh encompasses culture, politics and the social when studied from the perspective of tawaifdom. From the exchange of letters amongst patrons, promises made and broken in love, agreements and challenges faced during performances, Begum Samru assumes a more "national"[15] role. The interpersonal

---

[15] The concept of a nation or a nation-state did not exist

relationships that one sees within the kotha assume a broader scale with Begum Samru. The entire system of exchange of letters, trade, maintaining accounts of state expenditures that re-defines the female valuation under a new light. As a consequence, Begum Samru gets further desexualized and excluded from the domain of the erotic and the direct male gaze that the figure of the courtesan is deeply related to. But if one probes a little deeper, courtesans, in general, also nurtured some sort of marginality in pre-and post-Mutiny Lucknow. Even though the elites mingled with the sprouting industry of courtesans, the power center "allowed them to slide in and out of agency, control, and influence" (Feldman and Gordon, 6). This sets the center of the margin into a motion bringing in ambiguity to the aura that surrounded them.

> Courtesans can often take wealth and status away from their patrons as easily as they help generate it. Dialectically speaking, the rigid hierarchies of class and gender that allow courtesans to flourish make them powerful because they successfully challenge the delineations that keep received

---

prominently during Begum Samru's life. It was coined and used by Benedict Anderson's "imagined communities." The reference to nation here is used to assert a more pan-India view of Begum Samru's growing political dexterity.

social structures in place; but those same hierarchical social structures also deny courtesans full access to privileges guarded at the very highest strata of society. In all of these ways, courtesans and their arts are woven into a dynamic of privilege and constraint that forces a rethinking of the gendering of power. Their artistic practices become means of self-promotion—indeed self-preservation—within systems of freedom and oppression, which in turn involve them and their clients in high-level networks of social and political exchange. (Feldman and Gordon, 6)

Therefore, the courtesan culture had a symbiotic relationship with the rest of society, which shows the extent of its validation. It is clear that Begum Samru understood that politics and strategies could be extended into the public domain. This clearly makes the figure of the courtesan not the alternative of the wife but an institution in itself. This acted as an inverse principle that fuelled the British agenda of stigmatizing the courtesan culture. This idea was solely built on the fact that wealth created and circulated because of the courtesan culture was tainted and immoral. One can merely trace the origins of Begum Samru's personal life and find out as to how she ventured out politically.

It can be deduced that prostitution and sexual activity across cultures such as the ones that existed in Greece, Egypt, Japan, and India are interwoven with excesses in wealth, exoticism and glamour that also sustained the cult of the courtesans. Therefore, prostitution was an important "escape" for the sustenance of society. This escape can be defined in terms of recreation, pursuing of arts, metaphors of culture and the realm that could offer sexual pleasure that is necessary for the sustenance of society. Umrao Jan Ada and Begum Samru sprout in feudal Lucknow, both being the keepers of culture. While Begum Samru develops prominence through the *zenankhana*s of Reinhardt, Ruswa hints at Umrao's rather insignificant political presence in the court of Wajid Ali Shah (that of a nautch girl[16] who however can be viewed as a source full of potential). Both undergo a change of name but begum Samru's initiative to turn Christian as Joanna was more of a political attempt that helped her launch herself beyond the social, cultural, familial and national domain. She, then on, moved around with a larger circle of Catholics gathering more military and social prowess. This prompted her to maintain her foothold in India as well as amongst the British. "She represented herself alternately as a Muslim noblewoman, a Catholic aristocrat, a pious Christian and patron, and

---

[16] This is because by this time, as the novel approaches its end, Umrao is not shown to be operating from the kotha. Therefore, she can be defined as a nautch girl.

benefactor and benevolent ruler to the people of Sardhana" (Chakravarty, 155). As history chronicles it, she went on to prove her mettle in maintaining battalions in the court of Shah Alam during 1778 to 1788. Her battalions helped the Mughals save their skin and seek protection due to increasing threats from the Marathas, the Sikhs, the Rohillas and the Jats. She was felicitated by the Mughal emperor as Zeb-un-nissa that initiated her further into the Mughal nobility. The entire northern India was impressioned by her political presence and it was obvious that the Britishers would not have left her unnoticed. The *Calendar of Persian Correspondence* enlists:

> During this period, the Begum also came to the attention of the British: she helped secure the release of a young British officer who had been taken prisoner by Sikh chiefs. Major William Palmer, then resident in Gwalior, enlisted the Begum's help and her contribution was noted to the Governor General. (Chakravarty, 156)

This phase followed Begum Samru's marriage to a French nobleman and she turned Joanna Nobilis Somer. Curiously she still maintained her initial affiliation with Sombre that highlights her personal preferences (Ghosh, 156). At a later point in time, the changes in name almost mark the progression and diversification in her career establishing her aristocratic standing manifold.

It is interesting to note that she kept her Persian seal intact apart from using the new British seal, for political negotiations with the British.

After a series of political upheavals, between 1796 and 1803, Begum Samru turned more diplomatic in her approach towards the Marathas and the British. Later on, she joined the British services solidifying her political presence even further. According to historians, her marriage with the French nobleman has been erased and she now lives in the pages of history as Samru ki Begum.

Begum Samru was known for engaging her peers in conversations within the political circle and attending durbars cross-dressed. She often wore the turban along with trousers and stockings which created a sense of "cultural confusion" (Chakravarty, 160). Her Christmas feasts had nautch parties as well. Keeping this in mind, her inexhaustible taste for the Spectacle and the Performance cannot be denied. The fact that Begum Samru started her career as a nautch girl and was well known for her lavish nautch parties later in her political career, and her affinity and taste towards the courtesan culture conjoins both Begum Samru and Umrao at some level. The graph of being a woman and an entertainer reiterate:

1. The literary prowess
2. The political prowess
3. The physical prowess
4. The prowess of art

The figure of Umrao Jan allows us to discuss the metaphor of "performance" as a viable and meaningful life-defining symbol. A courtesan could be regarded as a living example of the performance of life and every nautch performance operated within the economies of desire. Focusing on high classical forms to light classical music such as dadra, tappa, thumri, tawaifdom unleashed energy in the heart of the classical orientation of North India. The desire underplayed itself at two levels:

1. A visible market place where the girls were bought and sold
2. A subtle economy of the courtesan's own desire

The second is the unspoken and an important thematic concern of the novel- Umrao's desire for economic and personal stability. Begum Samru and Umrao Jan seem to operate at the intersection of art and reality that highlight their "artfulness in everyday reality" (Feldman and Gordon, 35). This strategic bordering on the intersections of art and reality also highlight the politicization of aesthetics and aestheticization of politics (concept borrowed from Walter Benjamin) that made possible the easy flow of "desire" within the market structure and larger politics. Begum Samru's political success almost goes ahead to make her visible to the male gaze where the pricing of the body takes a backseat. She, no more, remains a commodity yet she nurtures her desires for political expansions and networking. Similarly, Umrao Jan Ada too, through her artfulness is able to aestheticize politics through her arts. Her songs almost become a *marsiya* to the Mughal rule in India, which is at its precipice, in the novel. Courtesans socialized with distinction of knowledge and arts and were not agencies that provided sex.

> By taking on such responsibilities themselves, courtesans could free their loving intercourse from the boring and desultory parts of life. (Bonnie and Feldman, 44)

The entire outlook towards the "calculating courtesan" to a "carefree amorous courtesan" (Bonnie and Feldman, 44) therefore, does not quite remain as a façade. The following is an extract from one of the incidents in Umrao's life as a courtesan:

> The servant bowed and left. My first thought was to call Bua Hussaini and show her the gold coins and ask her to give them to Khanum. Then I looked again at the glittering, newly minted money, and thought the better of it. Since I had no money-box of my own, I hid them under the foot of the bed. (Ruswa, 55–56)

The secreted money and the desire of being valued and loved is the essence of the conversation that follows this particular extract. During the conversation she compares Gauhar Mirza with the Nawab. But she cannot imagine a future with any of them. This signifies a double layer to this desire. This desire stands in contrast to the public rituals of desire that a courtesan must enact. The confession of wanting to be loved is a part of the public display of affection and which is different from the internal desire that cannot be made public. The fact that Umrao not loved anyone is based on the profligacy of love. Love no longer remains monogamous within the domain of tawaifdom. This spectacle of love is showcased during her conversation with Ruswa that takes place beyond formality and reserve. Umrao, at certain points of time in the text, seems to have fallen in love with the Nawab, Faiz Ali and Gauhar Mirza—men on whom she invested some imaging of the future. But in the last chapter she denies everything. This is the fundamental contradiction in her character that completes her role as a tawaif. She is the object of desire but can never be an autonomous subject of desire. This is why her life beyond the kotha cannot exist. This is a peculiar aporia[17]. This desire operates within the *bazaar* and can never become normalized because there can never be a return to the domestic space. Yet, the novel does not create a distinct male gaze. Umrao's "desire" that floats above the desire for loving men is larger than the immediate patriarchy that surrounds her. This is how an object which is innately known for her sexual capabilities gets desexualized in the process of deep understanding.

---

[17] A figure of speech expressing doubt or a conflict.

Now, let us look at Begum Samru and Umrao Jan Ada's life post their retirement. Umrao Jan Ada is no longer in the market. In the last chapter her debate highlights the difference between a virtuous chaste woman and a courtesan. It seems that her life was determined in ways that were beyond her control. She is shown to have been caught within the limited range of desires of the kotha and later on the court. One tends to feel that Ruswa becomes the last customer who will become the narrator of her life. The other end of the novel shows that people such as Khanum Jan and Dilawar Khan become the perpetrator of the system.

> I have some parting advice to those who follow my profession, and urge them to take heed of it. "My poor, simple prostitutes! Never entertain the false hope that any man will ever love you with a true heart. The lover who gives his body and soul to you will depart in few days. He will never settle down with you, and you are not even worthy of that. Only the virtuous, who see one face and never turn to another, will have the pleasure of true love. You, women of the street, will never find such a blessing from God. What was to happen to me happened. I am resigned to this and have fulfilled all my wishes. I have no desires left, though desire is a curse that never leaves you till your dying day. I hope that you will profit

from this account of my life. I end it with a
verse and hope for your prayer:

> *My dying day draws near. Perhaps, oh Life,*
> *My very soul has had its fill of thee."*

(Ruswa, 200)

In the above extract, it is difficult to decipher the
intention of the word "virtuous" as the narrator-author
conflict remains till the end. If Ruswa is Umrao's mouth-
piece then making a general plea for a woman's virtuosity
as a tool that only is available to women "who see one face
and never turn to another" is highly contradictory to the
entire drive of the courtesan culture. An erudite life of a
courtesan does not leave space for being virtuous as it is.
This is why they remain unfathomable. But ascribing the
qualities of being honourable and virtuous to women who
stick to the traditional notions of patriarchy and marriage,
does not seem like a comfortable idea tha Ruswa leaves us
with. What explains the presence of domnis who practiced
prostitution secretly within the walls of marriage? Can
they be called virtuous?

The Umrao Jan remains as an elegy to the bygone days
that is highlighted in Ruswa's interest in depicting the old
culture which thrives upon the separation between the
kotha and the haveli, the *purdah-nasheen* and the tawaif.
Toward the end of Begum Samru's career, her retirement
was respectful and ceremonious unlike that of Umrao's.
Begum Samru was assigned a tomb:

> On one side panel on the pedestal of this monument, the Begum was shown on her way to a durbar, atop a procession of elephants, further securing her historical stature as an important noblewoman. On another panel, the consecration of the church is depicted with the Begum handing a chalice to the archbishop. In death, as in life, Begum Samru evoked multiple cultural images... The renaming of Farzana, the dancing girl in Reinhardt's zenana, to Her Highness Joanna Zeb-un-nissa, Begum Samru implied much larger transformations than simply changing names. (Chakravarty, 163)

With Umrao Jan Ada, the audience sees a rather unceremonious farewell to the courtesans' way of life. Her lament in the end signifies the distaste that the Mutiny has left in the eyes of the culture that was once in its glory. In the end, she has visibly lost her legacy, her patrons and lives outside the premises of the kotha. So, a displaced woman is in contrast with Begum Samru. The courtesans post the 1857 Mutiny have been the highest tax payers, according to a sociological survey conducted by Veena Talwar Oldenburg in her essay "Lifestyle as Resistance: The Case of the Courtesans of Lucknow, India." It becomes evident that they were the immediate subjects of British castigation and moral denigration. With Begum Samru's rise in power, we realize that the cult of the courtesans formed an invisible power structure behind the operations of the throne. This political tradition therefore enjoyed a quiet involvement of the tawaifs.

> The Mughal government was a *kaghazi Raj*, a paper government. From the region of Akbar on, copies of all state communications were systematically preserved, along with a vast number of records and accounts, and the daily log of all that the emperor said and did. In the course of time, a mountainous pile of documents accumulated at the imperial capital. Unfortunately almost all of it was lost in the chaos of the eighteenth century, leaving only fragments in the provincial archives. (Eraly, 231)

From the Mughal perspective, the Europeans were more of traders than a political body. And the sea was not considered as the domain of the Mughals. For them, the land was the geographical and political domain. Therefore, around the 1850s, the Mughal Empire reached its precipice not being able to realize that the sea was the actual channel of more and more Britishers pouring in leading to annexation. This end also becomes the nemesis for Umrao's career as a tawaif. Umrao's poesy is now being read in relation to material production. Therefore, the mehfil or the musha'irah that was based on exchange of poetical gestures—a culturally produced symptom—now it is being used to ensure the operations of certain relations of mass consumption and transaction. This is symptomatic of many other Umraos that might have existed forming a collective body of art.

Umrao Jan Ada does not inherit any family tradition, hierarchical status or a cultural legacy. Her unwilling submission to the changing political process contributes to her personal failure. Also, towards the end she remains a distorted image of authority with only her maid servant taking care of her. This indicates that there has been a painful acceptance and internalization of the destruction. Or does it leave the readers with a window that will help us internalize it slowly and forever?

Begum Samru is Umrao's suitable counterpart in many ways but again the differences get established in the course of several arguments taken up in this chapter. *In Conversation with Gayatri Chakravarty Spivak* speaks about love and its validity brilliantly in one of the interviews in the text. She problematizes:

> Any *prem* is an irrational thing. This is what I was saying about law and justice. You actually work against—it's a conflict of interest, love is a conflict of interest. You can't base policy on love. (Spivak, 51)

Any literature discussing the life of a courtesan often faces the dangers of intermingling imagination with reality and gets conditioned by a firm belief of the readers that it is for entertainment. Therefore, the idea of "love" or "*prem*" within this non-conventional structure becomes even more subverted. The beauty of the courtesan and her prosperity depended on her charm, grace, passionate rendering of knowledge in conversations and the art of dance and music. Therefore, love becomes a "gesture" of demanding the patron's attention. This Space, therefore, becomes the perfect realm presenting a conflict of interest in love. The concept of love does call for a "home" or a "sanctuary" that would nurture feelings of the lovers. This is the precise policy of love. The kotha becomes a home away from home that encourages free love.

Umrao Jan Ada might be a novel that shows a failed revolution in terms of the overpowering British influence that the Mughal nawabs and kings could not cope up with, but Begum Samru's case study is highly symptomatic of a native woman educated in Englishness went beyond the immediate constraints of love, race and nativity issues. One cannot deny that the kothas were the arch structures of power that had women who could politically manipulate decisions made by nawabs and kings. It nurtured the interests of the elites and in turn received its patronage. In a way, the kotha was one of the prime agencies to contain and nurture the political structures. It also propagated the "borrowing" and "replaying" of the pretended reality of the patrons- a world where everything was ideal and maintained by women. The Britishers were quick to

83

"commodify"[18] the courtesans or nautch girls and keep them for "useful projects" such as maintaining harems, keeping native women as concubines and British soldiers visiting kothas. What Begum Samru must have realized is that these ideas had seeped into the British psyche which was evident from their wearing of native clothes, constructing Indian style bungalows with a zenana etc. Also, Jean Genet's idea of the political and the social come from the fact that "the innermost fantasies (of men and women) are both- sexual and political" (Genet, 20). Every fantasy or an imagination comes with a dominating subject and the ruler of the subject and there can be inversions in gender constructions as well. Therefore, the desire to rule or be ruled within the imagination brings along the political desires of the individual as well. Begum Samru's private life cannot be mirrored exactly within this argument with certainty but one can draw impressions of what the power structure would have been like. Her knowledge envelops political, military, religious, and bureaucratic power.

The zenana and the kotha were important spaces where "exchanging information, hearing gossips and

[18] Ideas borrowed from Genet (2005) is one of the most critiqued and noted playwright who is known for his unorthodox and subversive avant garde plays. He was himself a homosexual prostitute and was politically linked with Black Panthers and Palestinians for uplifting the marginalized.

conducting negotiations" (Ghosh, 75) was integral to its sustenance. Even though the difference between a kotha and the zenana become difficult to reconcile under one roof, but the above stated functions highlight a common agency that the women shared. Both these systems were necessary for the smooth running of the imperial realm and the circulation of wealth amongst household women and generate independent wealth for the courtesans (e.g., courtesans could extract or demand gifts that they could keep to themselves and give the rest of the payments to the *chaudharayan*). This larger political culture joined the Company servants, the local rulers and the natives.

The narratives of Palmer, Begum Samru and Umrao Jan Ada demonstrate the ways in which power structure worked its way out starting from the kotha to a larger national political domain. With Umrao, it was more of a private struggle for power and status (her relationships with her patrons, her relationship with Khanum Jan and her decayed relationship with her natal house); with Begum Samru the struggle for power and wealth, post Reinhardt's death gathers a larger momentum. The contradictions and ambivalences expressed in Umrao's and Begum Samru's case seem to have been complicated by "concerns about social opportunities, class status and cultural competence" (Chakravarty, 105), these still form the texture of the Mughal Era validating that even the most multicultural of men faced threats or closed-minded concerns when it came to understanding women.

Works Cited

"Plutocracy." Web. 30 May 2012 <http://en.wikipedia. org/wiki/Plutocracy>.

A Lady's Diary of the Siege of Lucknow. Delhi: Rupa & Co., 2002.

Chakravarty, Gautam. *The Indian Mutiny and the British Imagination*. Delhi: Cambridge, 2005.

Eraly, Abraham. *The Mughal World*. Delhi: Eastern Book Corporation, 2007.

Feldman, Martha and Bonnie Gordon. *The Courtesan's Arts: Cross-cultural Perspectives*. USA: Oxford University Press, 2006.

Genet, Jean. *The Balcony*. Ed. B. Mangalam. Delhi: Worldview Publications, 2005.

Ghosh, Durba. *Sex and the Family in Colonial India: The Making of Empire*. Cambridge: Cambridge University Press, 2006.

Hunt, Lynn. *Eroticism and the Body Politic*. London: Johns Hopkins University Press, 1992.

Oldenburg, Veena Talwar. "Lifestyle as Resistance: The Case of the Courtesans of Lucknow, India." *Feminist Studies* 16. 2 (Speaking for Others/Speaking for Self: Women of Color) (Summer, 1990): 259–87. Web. 30 May 2012. <http://links.jstor.org/sici?sici= 0 0 4 6 - 3 6 6 3 % 2 8 1 9 9 0 2 2 % 2 9 1 6 % 3 A 2 % 3 C 2 5 9 % 3 A L A R T C O %3E2.0.CO%3B2-A>.

Ruswa, Mirza Mohammad Hadi. *Umrao Jan Ada: Courtesan of Lucknow.* Trans. David Matthews. New Delhi: Rupa & Co., 2007.

Shreeve, Nicholas. *Dark Legacy: The Fortunes of Begam Samru.* Calcutta: Rupa & Co., 1998.

Spivak, Gayatri Chakravorty. *Conversations with Gayatri Chakravorty Spivak.* Calcutta: Seagull Publications, 2006.

CHAPTER THREE

THE SILENCED "SIRENS" AND THE EXTINCTION OF A CULTURE

Meri Lao's essay, *Sirens: Symbols of Seduction*, says

> More generally, courtesan's voices, capable of ensnaring men, were frequently associated with sirens, recalling the mythological half-bird/ half-woman creatures whose irresistible chants offered erotic pleasure by bewitching mortal men and forever detaching them from reason.

(Gordon and Feldman, 185)

According to Greek mythology, the word "sirens" is a folkloric representation of the female who were half-bird/half-woman creatures. They were known to lure men by their mysterious music and enchanting voices taking them to the midst of rocks and cliffs. These sirens were responsible for many shipwrecks as well. Such a representation contributes to the notion of the woman as the femme fatale and other such evil connotations. Several other authors, one being Homer, mentions the word sirens in their works hinting at women. According to the *Oxford English Dictionary,* a siren is:

1. A device for making a loud prolonged signal or warning sound
2. Each of a number of women or winged creatures whose singing lured unwary sailors on to rocks
3. A temptress; a tempting pursuit

Taking the third meaning and discussing it with reference to the courtesan-question, the events in the life of a courtesan might be distinct at every stage, age and level, but the representation of those events continues to be stereotyped in terms of its verbal and visual meanings. The term courtesan has been subsumed under the category of prostitution and sex-trade which is a blanket term and does great disservice to the specialized mode of life that the courtesans led. The word siren means a promiscuous and loud woman who is dangerous enough to lure men with her charm and musical skills. In this context, even though, Franz Kafka's short story *The Silence of the Sirens* is a much later version using the mythical siren creatures and their infectious songs[19], this short story weaves the siren-metaphor brilliantly for readers. Ulysses during his journey closes his ears and ties himself up to the mast of the ship to prevent the "attack" coming from the siren's song. However, Ulysses does not realize the fact that the silence of the sirens can be deadlier than their song. Upon unblocking his ears, he realizes that the sirens were silent all the time. This includes two possibilities:

1. Ulysses knew that the sirens were silent and pretended to take that extra precaution
2. Ulysses was sceptical about turning mad at the hands of the sirens.

---

[19] The metaphor of women singing songs occur in Indian literature also in a Tamil text *Cilappatikaram* (one of the five great epics of Tamil literature written in fifth century A.D.) wherein the love songs sung by Matavi (a figure who is linked to the arts of Madurai) and Kovalan near the seaside grove lead to misunderstandings in love. However, these songs sung on the lute are written according to the conventions of *sangam* poetry. The poems of *Cilappatikaram* are cryptic in nature and are ambiguous in their meanings. Not to say that Matavi is a siren-like figure in the epic but the presence of the songs signify the nature of ambiguity it can carry.

Kafka towards the end of the story admits that human understanding is deeper than one can possibly think but one should not waste oneself in futile interpretations and complicated approach to solving problems.

> Now the Sirens have a still more fatal weapon than their song, namely their silence. And though admittedly such a thing has never happened, still it is conceivable that someone might possibly have escaped from their singing; but from their silence certainly never. Against the feeling of having triumphed over them by one's own strength, and the consequent exaltation that bears down everything before it, no earthly powers could have remained intact. (Kafka, 431)

The last line of the extract needs to be probed into deeply. The entire ideology of associating women with something mythical and with its presence "no earthly powers could have remained intact" does not remain a Greek allusion any more. The interpretation has gathered many layers to it post several historical changes, one being the Mutiny of 1857. The Kafka-esque essence leaves a trail of the oft-repeated fact that the will of the (male) Self somehow fails to keep up in front of these "sirens" no matter how strong the resistance might be. Keeping the above context in mind, this gives rise to the pun that the word siren carries: if the women are the ones who raise alarm at impending dangers, why does the term siren then carry a negative connotation? The courtesans in Lucknow steer the era to its peak and help it get noticed in its entirety, wealth and glory with their musical arts, *adab* and political insights. The courtesans thus, formed the real material and cultural voices of the Mughal age. In short, the rituals of the tawaifdom were rich and influencing but its understanding in the eyes of the West became very reductive and limited. Therefore, treating the courtesan culture as the culture of the pre- and post-Mutiny Lucknow as the harbingers of vulnerability, unsteadiness and disease becomes a narrow observation. Siren, as the term denotes, means an alarm bell or something that gives out the distress signal in during troubled times. But the question is that if tawaifdom was about spectacle and art, then labelling the courtesan culture as the culture of excesses and licentiousness give us an extremely settled belief on the bygone culture. The purpose of the analysis is to highlight a new dimension to it that would qualify the term "siren" along with its strengths. In the lines quoted above from Kafka's short story, during Ulysses' journey, the song of the sirens cannot be heard by him that makes the sirens irresistible. In fact, what Kafka proposes is that the general human experience does not always get communicated smoothly with words and language. Therefore, there is always a problem of intelligibility that makes the process of communication complex. In the short story, the purpose of Ulysses' journey is not mentioned and the meeting between the sirens and this Greek hero is factually (location, time, setting) not supported. The story evokes the imagination of the readers despite the visible lack of physical description in the plot. The encounter is communicated well, still. Ulysses meeting the sirens is the exact portrayal of the encounter between the world and the Self. This thoughtful exploration does give rise to and sustain the ambiguities related to the term "sirens," even though that is not the author's immediate point of reference. By leaving the interpretation to be completed at the reader's disposal, the focus therefore, does not only remain within the World and the Self but also layers further into the term siren. In the end, Ulysses is successful in escaping them. One can possibly discuss the reason and logic behind the silencing of such sirens by Ulysses' act of shutting his ears but the focus on their condition post the deliberate and forced silencing share less attention.

The Silence of the Sirens is not an ordinary story. And ascribing it to the metaphor of a mythical creature is not enough, though it can be metaphoric as far as the thematic and the structural roots of the story are concerned. Double-edged satire does become the locus of the story. Here are a few observations that can help us integrate the question of the "siren" within the seams of my study. Sirens refer to the agents- the agents of destruction, messengers, the agents of the state, or even divisions of the mind which further accentuate the fear of the agents. The palpable state of human existence, in general, is what the Kafka-esque world depicts. This particular short story metaphorically implies the female agent which problematizes the identity-question further. The fact that the sirens of the sea were silent also highlights the other side of language that must be in existence and cannot be approached. The fact that the "unspeakable professions" are silent, in this context, reveals the other side of the written or the scriptable world. This kind of silence embedded within the universe poses both as a threat and as a liberation in Kafka. But the argument becomes complex when the cult of the courtesan is discussed. As in *The Country Doctor*, in *The Silence of the Sirens* also the meaning is thwarted. Doctor fails to understand the illness of the patient; similarly, the agents here are dumb and non-sensical in their attitude to convey the meaning. Therefore, the purposelessness of language and the silence in both the short stories is clearly brought out. Language is never static, but silence is. If language is for the people and the patriarchs in general, then the "minor" silencing has the potential to reclaim its politics and identity question.

Apart from that, one can draw resonances from the metaphor of half-bird/ half-woman creatures singing in the middle of the sea with the courtesan figure and her association with the art of song. Light classical songs such as *dadra*, *thumri*, and *tappa* caused enchantment in the listeners forcing them to choose love over reason and doubt which can be interpreted as a layer of the intelligibility and artfulness. The mehfils were known for causing "destructive pangs of love" (Feldman and Gordon, 185) amongst the patrons and were popular. The courtesans of the Mughal Age in India carried the cultural burden of Lucknow and were socially and politically influential. If courtesanship is defined

> as a social phenomenon whereby women engage in relatively exclusive exchanges of artistic graces, elevated conversation, and sexual favours with male patrons…(then) the artistic currencies is understood in their own cultural contexts to be wholly interdependent with their commerce in sex (Feldman and Gordon, 5),

then the threat that comes from the cult of the courtesans is the threat they held out to the domestic sphere that includes both the male and the female. In a way, one can say that the cult of the courtesan was a barometer for measuring the perils and the highs of the Mughal Age, in terms of political influences, prosperity, cultural advancements and incest. If this idea is understood as an inverted pyramid, then the courtesans who claimed to have the knowledge of literature and a deep understanding of culture, according to modern readings, are women who have already "transgressed." However, one fails to see that only the transgressed know the true nature of transgression. Therefore, the ways of life of the courtesan remain inaccessible to scholars and critics as they did play a major role in forming the court politics, influence the law of the state and help the nawabs take decisions. The courtesan figure, therefore, remains poised on Victorian doubts and historical changes.

The Victorian sentimentality had lashed out at the Indian lavish nautch parties by leading men astray. This change in taste that made the courtesans turn from cultural assets to objects of necessary evil was due to the violent and rapid transition. The Britishers insisted on their soldier's clinical hygiene. The Cantonment Act of 1864, seven years after the Mutiny of 1857, is self-explanatory. This Act shifted the courtesans not only close to the Regimental Bazaars but also labelled them as women having no taste, no time and no money, as documented by Oldenburg. This placed the regime of tawaifdom on the platform of "a venereal disease statistics" (Oldenburg, 138). The Britishers called the kothas *nishatkhana*s (literally meaning night houses or night clubs) that further narrowed the scope of their profession. The Cantonment Act included the following regulations:

1. Interference in cleanliness of the place
2. Tawaifs who were minors when they came of age would be permitted to marry
3. Tawaifs were issued certificates and tickets as a marker of their identity. These certificates were attested by the government and renewed periodically and carried a note in Urdu, Persian, and English stating that she was free from any venereal disease.

This came as a setback to the courtesan way of life, which earlier had its own aura of power and mystique and could lay claim to being the storehouse of elegance and sophistication which was also commercially viable. Oldenburg in her book *The Making of Colonial Lucknow* discusses one of the letters sent out by the British officials to the newspapers. It reads:

> Prostitutes who refuse registration on the pretext that they intend to lead transformed lives only to do so to evade the law by moving to another town. Such women should be branded on the chin, cheek, or forehead of their beautiful faces…If this is considered excessive, then their wrists should be branded. If a prostitute marries on a temporary basis [*mutah*] then the brand mark should be underlined [with a straight line] so that she may no longer be mistaken for a low [*neech*] woman. It is essential that the women are branded to save the respectability [*izzat*] of innocent men. (Oldenburg, 139)

The slapping of a degrading discourse to the courtesan way of life and their potential threat to the *izzat* is another way in which they have been silenced. The song and the dance recital formed an important currency of the tawaif that was meant to repay the patron's favour of showering her with "gifts." Apart from that, conversations with patrons led to sex that was treated as problematic in the eyes of the British. The courtesan's mastery of the art of sex and pedagogic discourses drew patrons and their heirs to learn the arts of *adab* from them with finesse. This formed a broader cultural and social context of the Mughal society in India. But how could one avoid the dangers of shifting the power of "being social and cultural symbols" to the courtesans? The reduction in visiting and patronising the kotha by branding the women associated with it was therefore, a mere economical stint. Courtesans cannot be the social arbiters. This silenced the industry and the arts forever.

Very few insights have been shared by historians and critics who have researched upon and recorded the culture of the courtesans, on the licensing and the policing that have gone into this forceful silencing of the sirens. The post Mutiny ruptures led to the silencing of the Lucknow courtesans and their eventual fading out from the scene never to return. The Indian Contagious Disease Act was passed in 1865 eight years after the Mutiny that helped the government put into effect strategies maintaining tight control on the tawaif culture of Lucknow. This meant that the courtesans were checked regularly on the basis of hygiene. This also marks the emergence of the welfare state where the flourishing economy under the British rule and the decaying nawabi Raj was closely formulated and structured. Several institutions that acted as the political centers were formed which were aimed at social and moral policing of the natives. This also included placing a ban on institutions that practiced the kotha culture. The psychological impact of such a social upheaval forces us to travel deep in the subjective interiors of the minds of the courtesans. The cult of the courtesan was rich in techniques of poetical and expressive language, music, dance, everyday conversations and etiquettes of personal dialogue. The courtesan culture was put to a psychological death as is exemplified in the stories of Umrao Jan Ada, Begum Samru and Gohar Jan. For example, a smile is seen as a natural reciprocation of happiness when seen in sync with feelings. Otherwise, the smile gets dis-connected when seen in isolation. Similarly, the ruptures within the courtesan culture due to strict licensing by the Britishers, appeared more like a disconnect that was seen in isolation when its meaning was aligned with prostitution rather than seeing it as the courtesan ideology. The suspension of the institution of courtesanship from the mainstream culture of the Mughals might be the possible reason for its derogatory interpretation. During the licensing, the propertied class of nawabs were also dislodged from their financial prowess overnight. Such a change directed the flow of money from the established courtesans to the British authorities.

Veena Talwar Oldenburg, during her interview-session with an aging courtesan of Lucknow Gulbadan, writes in her seminal essay 'The Case of the Courtesan of Lucknow- India' that "because society has virtually denied women control over wealth and property, it is essential to establishing a countercultural way of life" (275). Oldenburg reports

> Gulbadan said she often carried the game a step further by "allying" herself with the patron against the "offending" courtesan to set the seal of authenticity on the scene. She would scold and even slap her till the patron begged her not to be so harsh. Gulbadan was the privately acclaimed champion of these more serious confidence tricks and others cheerfully confessed to having blackmailed, stolen, lied, and cheated for material gain as soon as they acquired competence in this art. (Oldenburg, 275)

Such severe licensing and moderating of the courtesan way of life not only started the slow and steady erosion of the nawabi culture of Lucknow but also ruptured the existing finances of the Mughals in India and forced the courtesans to switch to lowly manners practiced by roadside prostitutes. Words used by Gulbadan such as "cheated for material gain," "blackmailed," "stolen," "lied," etc., signify the vulnerability of the courtesan-industry that might not have been equipped to acclimatize to major social changes. The Mughal age did cater to major flow of money in and outside the kotha structure that, to an extent, acted as liberation for the female lineage (women who worked as courtesans). This exact autonomy was treated as a sexual excess in the eyes of the British. The reasons they gave were largely hygienic, moral and social in nature. However, we can today express our dismay on the pompous and self-opinionated manner of the white colonizer which misread the Indian way of life, time and again causing permanent harm to the harmonious composite fabric of Mughal India.

As Gulbadan recalls, the economic rupture impacted the courtesan's arts right in their roots of cultural existence and learning. The British agenda prioritized the growth of their regiment basecamp in Lucknow and wished for their safety from venereal diseases. In the above extract, Oldenburg's findings give us an insight into the Space of courtesans in comparison with cultural distortions that brought in the heterogeneity in understanding the word tawaif. Interestingly, a sort of moral policing by the Britishers also spread in the city that expounded on the idea of being respectable and chaste which seemed as a logical extension of the Victorian sentimentality. One can also see the prominence of ideas denying the Space of the courtesan within society in Calcutta as well, during the Nationalist Movement that propagated the concept of the *bhadralok* and the *bhadramahila*:

> The intrusion of the criterion of "moral character" had interesting repercussions on the wives and other female relatives of the ex-king. Those "females of the family," who were "well-known" to be "unchaste,"

101

"addicted to vicious pursuits," or "notorious characters" were dropped from the original lists of pensioners. (Oldenburg, 202)

As historical accounts go, the emergence of the Company undermined the power of the nawabs at a steady pace and in several ways. Towards the end of the twentieth century, even the nawabi armies that were maintained by the British were poorly paid and not well-maintained. Wajid Ali Shah's initial imprisonment at Qaisarbagh by the Britishers showed that the Mughal activities were discouraged severely. Therefore, they ultimately became voluntary prisoners in their own capital. As Rosie Llewellyn-Jones observes in *The Tales of Old Lucknow*, the annexation was not a sudden imperial whim. Wajid Ali Shah's shabby treatment by the Britishers and protracted threats from Kolkata (the seat of Britishers) about the annexation was a signal good enough predicting the future course of events. Post the annexation, Wajid Ali Shah was sent away to Kolkata from where he kept sending pleas to the Company worrying about his property and kingdom. Lucknow was visibly demolished. Wajid Ali Shah was forced to abandon the city of Lucknow and all his property was taken over by the British officials. Not only did Wajid Ali Shah lose his hold on the land but all the *taluqdars* and *jagir*s working under his regime faced the brunt of a major sociopolitical change.

The leaving of the British from Lucknow was far less dramatic than their coming. On the surface the city seemed very different from that first entered by the British in February 1856, lost the following year and re-captured the next. Lucknow's status had initially suffered a reverse in 1877 when Awadh was amalgamated with the North-Western provinces, and the capital shifted to Allahabad, but Lucknow rallied at the turn of the century and re-established itself as the symbolic centre in political, cultural and religious terms. It was no longer isolated geographically the development of the railway complex in the former Nawabi garden of Charbagh, to the south of the city, made Lucknow an important junction. The bridging of the Ganges at Cawnpore in 1872, replacing the old crossing of boats, eventually linked Lucknow to Calcutta. (Jones, 155)

Wajid Ali Shah, the last ruler of Awadh, was officially relieved of his duties in a notice release by the British government that acted as a major blow and marked a stark period of change to the courtesan way of life. They were the evolving victims of their once-established and prospering profession. There is a dearth of existing records of the women themselves who practiced this art that have been recorded by Oldenburg and a few international authors. As

Pierre Corneille, a French dramatist, in his essay 'Women, Stereotypes Of' rightly states that the human nature takes a lot of voyeuristic "pleasure in looking for a vice or fault behind a quality" (1). This association of meanings can be traced from hussy to witch to a prostitute. Terms like hussy (a saussy or an impudent girl that was used in Middle English), witch (a woman endowed with magical powers women who practice sorcery) and a prostitute (who sells sex for money) have shown a direct silencing of women with range of terms that define the gender at large in a negative light. Such interventions that mark the body and the gender of the woman into stereotyped norms come from patriarchal formations. These patriarchal formations have to be pushed aside to question and investigate what led to the labelling of courtesans or courtesan-like women as sirens. Women have faced some sort of displacement at some level or the other that mark their detachment from the Self. Even the *byahta* model asks for a customized conformist living with the patriarchy. Patriarchy as a norm is much more defined and established in relation to the emerging concepts of matriarchy and feminism. Other models such as matriarchy, motherhood and the like are also seen in terms of the emerging trends on feminism and not a lot of these concepts seem to stand on their own, like the way patriarchy does. This displacement is found in *Umrao Jan Ada* very evidently. Umrao is abducted in her childhood. This symbolizes a multi-layered displacement. Her abduction was not within her control and shows the limitless power of the patriarchy and what it can do to make emerge stronger. On the contrary, her abduction put her into a much larger power structure, which was playing a major social, political and economic role in the Mughal Era, in general. This was something the colonizers could not fathom. As the historical pattern goes, we see that a "siren" has to be silenced because of the threat the patriarchy faces.

Silencing was a deliberate strategy on the part of the colonizers, in general. Any traditional patriarchal society in India has followed a strict moral code of conduct where the ways of expressing sexuality and sexual relations were kept under the caustic eye. Similarly, certain domains such as the *byahta* model and the woman (who is not a courtesan) is categorized as the *lakshmi* or *saubhagyawati*. She is supposed to hold on to the strings of domesticity and blesses the house with a prosperous wedlock. On the other hand, the exclusion of the courtesan from this canon places them within a silent zone, of sorts. While patriarchy serves to regulate the silences of the married women, he courtesan figure can be viewed as marginalized and silent. Interestingly, though, that was not quite the case in pre-modern or pre-British policy that impacted cultural centers like Lucknow, Delhi, or Calcutta. Rather, the courtesan or the courtesan-like existence, despite all the boundaries that kept her out of the domestic "blessed space," was empowered in nuanced ways and made a definite difference to the sociopolitical scene. She, therefore, had a voice, which the colonizer sought to silence in the interest of the narrow-minded Calvinistic morality.

Words such as rand and randi describe a widow or a sterile woman. The very fact that any civilization has space and terms to accommodate both the categories of woman ironically outline the fact that the two categories are interweaved. The pure-model of woman has the "potential" to transgress and therefore the second category stands prepared for a cold-hearted welcome of the fallen woman. It must be pointed out that the sexual potential of the woman is therefore, imagined and constructed much in advance by patriarchy. In other words, the chaste woman has the prospect to turn into a spectacle of prostitution. This is exactly where the silencing starts.

The courtesan's agency lies within the domain of art, music, culture and dance that determines their economic inflow. The consumers of this art are the patriarchy and the contributory artists within the kotha structure also largely consisted of Ustads and Gurus. Therefore, the agents who produced music and the agents who sustained them as patrons belonged to patriarchy. In such a cultural discourse that we see in Mughal India, the term siren seems not very apt for the courtesan figure. Therefore, this unequal battle between the individual agency of the courtesan figure and the collective constraint of the society is the disturbing cause that led to its extinction.

It is interesting to note that the definition of a siren and its affected meanings work from within a Space that is discussed below:

1. This Space that sustains the courtesan structure is autonomous. After a certain point, the sustenance of the courtesan becomes independent of the kotha she works for. She has the right to choose her patron though she has to work through this Space of negotiations that it offers.

2. This Space is not a cultural void. The rise and the fall of the Mughal Empire were very much reflective of the existence of the courtesan culture and tawaifdom. When the Mughal Empire was at its peak, the activity influenced this space but the space seemed to be gathering a power of its own that worked its way through the patriarchy and its resistance. It was only after an external disturbance that the opulent structure of the kotha suffered setbacks.

3. This Space coined the word tawaif that was not universal but cultural. This was more specific to the Indian context. The later day version termed as a "prostitute" seems much more universal that can accommodate women from all categories and positions. The term tawaif originated as an Arabic word *taifa* who were known to cater to the nobility of South Asia[20].They were known to master the nuances of music, dance, and Urdu literature. The noble gentry sent their sons to the

---

[20] http://en.wikipedia.org/wiki/Tawaif. Last visited on 12 May 2012

kothas for social training in literature, etiquettes, and *adab*. When most of the household women were illiterate, tawaifs were the only ones who were highly educated. In the coming years post Mutiny, this term seems to have conflated a variety of meanings, even though there was a strict hierarchy that the Mughals followed. The randis and the bazaari randis were available for easy sex trade but the tawaifs were highly skilled women who were politically aware and were well-versed in the literary realm too. Modern day terms such as sex workers or even women who are declared promiscuous at some level or the other are called as prostitutes that make the school of the kotha-culture suffer at the hands of the modern day perils. In other words, the term tawaif has been highly misconstrued.

4. This Space perfectly synchronized the existence of the pleasure factor, the fear factor and the imagination factor when it comes to witnessing and understanding the courtesan's way of life. This is why this sSpace is self sustaining. Even though one sees a sad demise of the Mughal Empire at the hands of the British, this sSpace exists at some level within the mind of every individual—man or a woman. Currently, this space sustains itself in a much more diluted manner where it tends to lose its power of being an empowered solitary body and is prone to the subjugation of the masses.

Eroticism and seduction that was a part of the *kotha* culture occupied only a minute domain of the entire school of thought that existed in the Mughal Age. Post the Mutiny of 1857, the common perception of the tawaif culture was limited to unidirectional beliefs that highlighted the illegitimacy behind this institution.

Post independence, this space diluted into the mainstream that brought in the musical revolution through the All India Radio and Shellac records. This gives rise to one question: in such a patrilinear structure did the courtesans at all have a matrilinearity? Apart from that, post the Mutiny and the annexation of Awadh and the abolishing of the existent feudal courts, why did the kotha structure waver to such an extent that it became hard for them to "reproduce" their profession into the changes that were brought in by the society? In order to address these questions, I would like to problematize the courtesan's individual agency. As an agency, this has the tendency to gather an entire gamut of negative connotations with it. The diminishing agency of the courtesan seems more of extrinsic erosion rather than an intrinsic turmoil. The problem of assimilation of meanings of terms ascribed to the courtesan way of life does not seem coherent 1850s onward. Also, the reader both reconciles and fails to reconcile with the text *Umrao Jan Ada* and its dual narration. Through the lens of Umrao Jan, one does not find a quality of opacity which is accessible to us in the first reading of the text. But the underlying cause seems hard to penetrate. With Umrao's narrative we see the narrative rigoured with nearly three hundred odd years of literary culture. Her changing narrative tone shifts the burden to the readers who are accountable for deciding the usefulness of the insights given out by the ageing courtesan. This new engagement with the courtesan's ethnography and psychology makes us rethink the term siren that is used pejoratively against this cult. The need to construct a unidirectional world of the courtesan way of life is necessary but the integral logic of the narrative as well as the turmoil that Lucknow witnesses offers no restoration except for the last line:

My dying day draws near. Perhaps, oh Life,
My very soul has had its fill of thee. (Ruswa, 200)

This sanctifies the extinction of the culture as the courtesan way of life and its old confidence was shattered with new values. This disintegration of the courtesan way of life, the fading cultural grandeur, the Mughal political foothold and literature that existed from the sixteenth century to the nineteenth century probably constitutes the dramatic voice of Umrao Jan.

In other words, the Space of Lucknow that encouraged the courtesan culture remained the same but the context changed. The colonial expansion and its encounter with Lucknow make the city appear like a pack of cards that is being constantly reshuffled to rewrite history. If history and culture shift and have a tendency to rearrange their inclinations and doubts, then it should have been a viable possibility that the cult of the courtesan should have resurfaced credibly at a later point in time. Rather, its existence today is negatively discussed and treated as a topic that can be spoken about only in private spaces and hushed tones. From an inverted point of view, just as the private space makes the general space visible, the existence of the kotha-structure in contrast to the usual domestic model becomes a reason for perpetration of terms like the siren. The following extract from Ghosh's *Sex and the Family in Colonial India* supports the point being discussed:

> Frequently published accounts of social life in India were repetitive, almost formulaic, showing the process of constructing Britishness in India. Native women are thus often represented, when they do appear, as threats to Britishness precisely because they disrupted the picture of appropriate social and cultural life in the colonial settlement, which was frequently represented as the "whitened" social space of mansions, grand balls, and horseback riding. (Ghosh, 37)

This domestic model might not necessarily be an Indian model. The British model also faced equal threat from the sexual license that the state of Awadh gave to

111

its courtesans. During the British intervention in India (1600–1780), especially the first phase, "the image of a European man and a native woman living in familial harmony has long been an enduring vision of colonial societies" (Ghosh, 1). But the moral, social and the political space of India did not agree with the British mind set for long and it led to accusations. Ghosh writes,

> although conjugal relationships between the European men and native women were commonplace in many colonial settlements on the Indian subcontinent, cohabiting with or marrying a native woman was often regarded as a socially and sexually transgressive act, one that gave rise to multiple types of regulation. In spite of the image that men who participated in interracial sex were socially enlightened and cosmopolitan, European men often kept these relationships secret, revealing them only in final wills and testaments. (Ghosh, 3)

Therefore, there were sufficient doubts and hesitation amongst the British people in "going native." The fact that the Britishers did not want to assimilate well into the Indian culture and therefore did not regard the Indian marital domain highlights that they saw it as something which was illegitimate. Within this ideology, the tendency to keep concubines in harem-like arrangements seems natural in every respect. The native women's properties, in the 1800s, were structured according to the British patriarchs who were, at a later stage, totally shaken due to the spread of venereal diseases. Thus, if we are talking about a transition in Lucknow and the British treatment of Lucknow, we see that the transition never happened. The mind set was already divided to the vein, like any other "usual" colonial venture and conquest, and it was the limitation of the act of assimilation that the Indian sentimentality failed to notice. The crisis that Lucknow faced more vividly toward the beginning of the nineteenth century affected the way of life of the courtesans who were the "interconnecting link" between politics, domestic, social and the economic space and the Mughal reign. Any kind of silencing is unnatural. This implies that not all courtesans who existed suffered the brunt of historical shifts and faced severe economic crises had the chance to voice their angst within the pages of history. Even though Oldenburg records several instances of courtesans in several of her sociological studies that inscribe the voices of the courtesans and their living conditions in the twentieth century, it still fails to capture and solidify a more solid body of literature. Scarcity of such accounts lead to assumptions about the bygone culture of the courtesan and make it more penetrable with meanings and interpretations. Also, through Umrao's voice the narrative potential foregrounds her considerably bringing her into direct contact with the readers. This potential heightens the power to be desired even within the pages of the book where the performativity seems scripted within words of the author-narrator. This agency is available with Umrao Jan but is missing from the body of courtesan literature at large. This too is a level of silencing that has happened post the Mutiny of 1857 in Lucknow.

What one fails to see is that the kothas provided the male gentry a space where the feudal structure got diluted to a great extent. As Regula Burckhardt Qureshi discusses in her essay "Female Agency and Patrilinear Constraints" in *The Courtesan's Arts: Cross-Cultural Perspectives*:

> The tawa'if's independence was indeed singled out in contrast to respectable women suffering from male oppression, but such independence could not pass the test of Victorian social norms. Already by the late nineteenth century, tawa'if and their dance became morally stigmatized by the "anti-nautch" movement of missionaries and middle-class social reformers. Half a century later, nationalist musical reformers simply followed suit, with the aim of replacing bad courtesans with good wives. (Faraone and MCclure, 319)

Thus, the essence comes through clearly. The courtesan culture manages to stand strong and undeterred as a profession and as a collective whole but its disintegration led to disempowerment. Such reforms introduced by the

Britishers was another form of silencing the woman at many levels, that left the cult of the courtesan break into still smaller power structures that could operate on a less significant scale in remote cities. This too was not possible in the late twentieth century across India. In *Beyond Clay and Dust*, the manner in which Gohar Jan is asked to vacate her premises that the Municipal officials declare it as "inhabitable" adds to the precision and the tapered intention of the colonial agenda. Had this culture proliferated then it would definitely have transgressed the patrilinear and class boundaries. The usual assumptions that govern such a patriarchal ideology (that can be conscious or an unconscious formation) are as follows:

1. Womanhood, motherhood, and tawaifdom (courtesans)—these remain as three distinct categories as far as the concept of chastity applies to itself. In the first two cases, the tendency of assumption diminishes or even stops after a certain point within the domain of the sexual. With tawaifs one witnesses an amplified imaginative possibility.

2. Secondly, the notion of the body/bawdy, its usage (political, social, and economical) and its resultant fate remain as crucial governing factors in case of the courtesan. The mother and the woman, in general, are not vulnerable to drastic environmental changes as they operate or are eligible to operate within the domestic sphere.

Courtesans being subjected to the usage of body and enter into the domain of the bawdy, they transgress the social very evidently making the cult more prone to imaginations and assumptions.

These were the factors that led to the sprouting of ideas making the culture-specific idea of the courtesan turn into an idea that was gathering layers of connotation post 1857. The disempowerment of the Nawabs was a reason that affected the tawaifdom to a considerable extent. The banishing of the patrons of popular courtesans had to be a direct consequence of British intervention and the extinction of such a school of thought in the later years. Musharraf Ali Farooqi in his novel *Between Clay and Dust* also locates two female characters on the brink of the twilight of the Nawabi Awadh. Gohar Jan and Malka observe the slow and steady fall in the number of patrons who visit her kotha. She is tight-lipped in the beginning of the novel and also lets Malka leave the confines of the kotha willingly with one of Malka's admirers. This being the first tragic blow in the novel that is revealed right at the beginning, the second wave of change comes out with the knowledge of Malka's marriage to her admirer, Hayat. Marriage is not an option for courtesans and the Malka-Hayat marriage synonymises a significant change. In an extract from the novel and almost after a week of Malka's farewell from the kotha, Banday Ali (the keeper of the kotha and the faithful accountant of Gohar Jan), not being able to keep his silence anymore and seeing Gohar Jan's drastic decisions and her cold heartedness towards Malka, breaks out in retaliation. He retorts:

> While handing Gohar Jan his monthly report on the kotha's finances, he confronted her.
>
> "If it was Malka's happiness you sought, surely you could see how happy it would have made her if you allowed her to perform. You never did."
>
> Gohar Jan silently looked through the accounts.
>
> "Not once, Gohar Jan," Banday Ali said. "You did not allow her to perform even once. You denied her all she had longed for since she was a child."
>
> Gohar Jan now looked up and met Banday Ali's angry gaze.
>
> "How could I, Banday Ali?" Gohar Jan said slowly, "How could I impose a destiny on her, or tie her to the kotha with any bonds? Don't you realize she was given to me in trust."
>
> With those words Gohar Jan finally answered every question Banday Ali had asked himself for the last twenty-three years on the subject of the girl who had been abandoned at the kotha's steps, and Gohar's treatment of her. (Farooqi, 46–47)

In this particular instance, Gohar Jan echoes certain characteristics of Umrao Jan Ada where both these courtesans adopt a certain heroic stance- Gohar's decision to free Malka from the confines of the kotha and Umrao's decision to leave Khanum's kotha. Farooqi highlights an interesting aspect in this conversation between Banday Ali and Gohar Jan. The denial of the performative space to Malka is indicative of the un-fulfilled role of the courtesan that Malka could have potentially become. Gohar Jan never allows her to "perform" which means that Malka faced adifferent level of silencing from within the kotha where she was raised from her childhood. Did Gohar Jan make Malka more of a "normal" woman who never was subjected to the direct male gaze of the man? Apart from that, Gohar Jan's deliberate silence on this issue considerably reduces the erotic factor (in relation to the male gaze and the eroticity of performance) that is associated with courtesans and brings out various levels of psychological death that the courtesan way of life experiences during the twilight of Lucknow. On the other hand, Umrao's silence is broken by Ruswa's insistence of penning down her life. Therefore, agencies such as Banday Ali and Ruswa participate within the zone of silences to break the silence. Another instance from *Beyond Clay and Dust*, upon Banday Ali's interrogation predicting Malka's return, Gohar Jan says:

> Gohar Jan spoke softly and reluctantly, as if uttering the words might make the dreaded

thing happen. "If she returned Banday Ali...
she could have what is not allowed any tawaif
in the same circumstances: she could have the
life she thought she wanted." (Farooqi, 47)

Even Umrao Jan's return to khanum's kotha does not provide her much. Though Ruswa tends to portray Umrao's return as just a *camera obscura* recording the changing times of Lucknow that Umrao did not experience first-hand, Gohar Jan's worry for Malka's return seems to have come from the strict codes of conduct practised inside the kotha that she wanted Malka to avoid. It is rightly said that the ways of the world can create possibilities for a woman to turn to tawaifdom but her sustenance might be questionable from time-to-time. This is the ultimate politicization of the aesthetics of the kotha structure that one needs to egage with. Umrao Jan Ada and Gohar Jan dictate a respect and erudition in their behaviour and manners. Umrao, on her return to Lucknow, sees that her former room has gathered dust and was full of cobwebs in Khanum's kotha.

The carpets of the room were turned back
and rubbish was strewn everywhere. What
a contrast from the old days, when my room
used to be so neat and tidy. It would be
swept four times a day, the bedding would be
regularly beaten, and not a speck of dust was
to be seen. Now I had no desire to sit there

> even for a moment, and when I looked at my
> bed, I had a feeling of disgust. (Ruswa, 174)

A similar instance can be found in Musharraf Ali Farooqi's *Between Clay and Dust*:

> It had adversely affected the fortunes of the tawaifs' enclave—a world that thrived on extravagance, and where people traditionally flaunted their wealth and fine taste.... The carpets had not been aired in a long time and were musty. In the music rooms, tanpuras gathered dust under their silken wraps and their necks became bent from the humidity.... The quiet of the music rooms was broken sometimes by the sound of a string snapping. (Farooqi, 27–28)

These instances not only show the emotional insights in the life of the courtesans but also make transparent the visible physical and geographical displacement and dilapidation. This is put forward by Kenneth Clarke's view on civilization, what constitutes it and what leads to its downfall. In his book *Civilisation: A Personal View*, Clarke is of the view:

> Vigour, energy, vitality: all the great civilisations- or civilising epochs- have had a weight of energy behind them. People

sometimes think that civilisation consists in fine sensibilities and good conversation and all that. These can be among the agreeable *results* of civilisation, but they are not what make a civilisation, and a society can have these amenities and yet be dead and rigid.

So if one asks why the civilisation of Greece and Rome collapsed, the real answer is that it was exhausted. And the first invaders of the Roman Empire became exhausted too. And so often happens, they seemed to have succumbed to the same weaknesses as the people they conquered. (Clarke, 21)

The Mughal rule from the sixteenth century till the late nineteenth century had a strong value system and an economic system that can be compared to the affluent cultures of Greek and Rome in terms of Mughal architecture, paintings, clothes, jewels, conquests, food and even the art of courtesans.

For a moment, if the British conquest is kept aside as an immediate reason for the Mughal Empire's downfall, then one does see the presence of extreme wealth, strong political networking in the Northern domain of India and an even greater cultural influence that gives us an idea about the culture being at its peak. As Clarke quotes Ruskin in *Civilisation: A Personal View*, Ruskin says: "Great nations write their autobiographies in three manuscripts, the book of their deeds, the book of their

121

words and the book of their art. Not one of these books can be understood unless we read the two others, but of the three the only trustworthy one is the last" (Clarke, 17–18). This concept can be applied to the Mughal society as well. The culture of the Mughals can be studied at par with the culture of the Greeks and Rome because of its architectural marvels, its art motifs, costumes and literature. If the deed-word-art factor is not applied to the culture of the Mughals in India, then the analysis does not hold together in its entirety. The project of colonising Indian geography came with the breaking of this three-tier chain into parts. The deeds of the Nawabs were segregated and the last Mughal ruler was sent away from Lucknow; the word of the plutocratic rule was not paid any heed to by the British officials even though their titles remained with them (which was ineffective); and the art and architecture of the Mughals in India which was the most popular way of expressing cultural feelings was destroyed by the British intervention. Apart from that, several Acts such as The Cantonment Act of 1864, The Indian Contagious Disease Act of 1865, the creation of the Lock Hospital and The Anti Nautch Movement were significant landmarks that obliterated the a major cultural references of the Mughal rule- the courtesan culture. A culture of a particular tribe or a sect survives not on the basis of geography but on the basis of cultural and oral traditions that are carried by the people. This very act of destroying the Mughal culture from its roots was evident from the severe moral and social policing undertaken by the British.

The introduction of Lock Hospitals in the city of Lucknow was damaging for the courtesan way of life. Lock Hospitals were first introduced in London to separate people having venereal diseases. This was usually located in the outskirts of the city meant to "isolate or quarantine" the infected people. Lucknow, post the 1857 insurgency, saw a heightened increase in the number of inspections for venereal diseases in the locals and the British regimented soldiers. These inspections did bring in a decrease in the occurrence of venereal infections but the slow and steady branding of the courtesans into petty prostitutes, the destruction of the baghs of Lucknow and the financial difficulties faced by the Lakhnawis increased. Lucknow, towards the beginning of 1900s saw a new day but pauperization was the new *adab* in the city of the rich Mughals. The colonial policy was aggressive and the city seemed different on the surface as well.

The relationship of the Mughals in India with the European kingdoms was on an entirely different plane from that of their relationship with Asian kingdoms. The power of the European states was unknown to the Mughals, and was made suspect by the slander and recriminations the agents of different European nations flung at each other—the Portuguese, for instance, consistently described the English as the petty nation of thieves.

The Mughals considered Europeans more as traders than as political or military entities. European powers no doubt dominated the seas, but as the Mughals did not consider the sea around India as part of their domain, they did not pay much attention to what went on there. (Eraly, 236)

Abraham Eraly's book *The Mughal World* gives a more definitive logic to the extinction of the cult of the courtesan. He analyses:

How did the great empire come to this whimpering end? Aurangzeb's theocratic policies, contrary to common perception, had little to do with it. By the end of his reign, Muslims had been ruling India for over 500 years, and many of their early rulers had been far harsher than Aurangzeb in their treatment of Hindus…. The main reason for the Mughal collapse was that the empire had grown far too large, beyond the capacity of the emperor to hold it together or to govern it efficiently. The administrative problems of the empire were compounded by its financial crisis, because of poor revenue collection on the one hand and the ballooning cost of government on the other. Moreover, the entire administration had become rotten to the core, shot through with corruption.... "It was inwardly decayed, and ready to fall to pieces as much by its own irrecoverable weakness, as by the corroding power of the Marathas," recorded Bhimsen, a courtier of Aurangzeb. (Eraly, 384)

This can be one of the governing reasons for the extinction of the Mughal Empire as such. Eraly's response to the extinction can be a probable reason as no empire stands perfect with respect to its governmentality. The administrative system was proven faulty towards the 1700s. In 1752, a treaty was signed that gave the Marathas the right to protect the Mughal throne. Marathas were the biggest threats for the Mughal Empire and Aurangzeb's death weakened the Mughal hold over the Indian subcontinent. Successive wars were fought and the Marathas fought the Mughals for twenty-seven years at a stretch. Religious intolerance amonght the Marathas and Muslims was at its peak and Mughals lost all their conquests in the Deccan region. In the year 1737, Nader Shah's attack on Delhi was a defining moment in history of Mughal Empire. He was successful in capturing the Peacock Throne following which every battle fought against the Marathas impacted the Mughals. By the time, Lucknow had survived the repeated defeats, Bahadur Shah Zafar II was exiled and sent away during the 1857 rebellion. Such a rupture was big enough for the Britishers to take advantage of. Their trade interventions from the sea not only studied the Mughal framework of approaching decadence but their agenda of colonization and modernization was implemented with a sense of urgency right after the 1857 rebellion. However, it is hard to absorb the total vanishing of the courtesan way of life and the culture and tradition that stitched the Mughal kingdom into one.

The universe is believed to be a phallocentric one but the agency of the female cannot be denied. In deconstructing the history of Lucknow, we do construct other histories- one of them being the history of the courtesan way of life. Ruswa penned Lucknow's history through Umrao Jan Ada. And the construction of the female Self within this class of women becomes a motive to not only discuss the unspeakable professions but also study in detail what sustained this school of thought. Courtesans gave birth to several forms of poesy, popularized Kathak and light classical music and became the central characters of literary representations. The purpose of my study was to define the practice and locate its validity within the Mughal reign.

Work Cited

Atikal, Ilanko. *Cilappatikaram: An Epic of South India.* Trans. R. Parthasarthy. New York: Columbia University Press, 1993.

Clark, Kenneth. *Civilisation.* London: BBC Books, 1969.

Eraly, Abraham. *The Mughal World.* Delhi: Eastern Book Corporation, 2007.

Faraone, Christopher A., and Laura K. McClure, ed. *Prostitutes and Courtesans in the Ancient World the University of Wisconsin Press.* Wisconsin: Monroe Street Madison, 2006. Web. 30 May 2012. <https://mail-attachment.googleusercontent.com/attachment/?ui=2&ik=c3570a1086&view=att&th=1374c19fab09c a1c&attid=0.9&disp=inline&realattid=f_h27f3xc112 &safe=1&zw&saduie=AG9B_P9KWrpXVNjYBltK KGhqF_4b&sadet=1338227823797&sads=1BVso2Iw 5tEg1o5i5u5i7vZ4A08>.

Farooqi, Musharaff Ali. *Between Clay and Dust.* Trans. David Davidar. New Delhi: Aleph Book Company, 2012.

Feldman, Martha and Bonnie Gordon. *The Courtesan's Arts: Cross-cultural Perspectives.* USA: Oxford University Press, 2006.

Illustrated Oxford English Dictionary. India: DK Publishers Illustration and OUP Publication, 2003.

Kafka, Franz. *The Complete Short Stories.* Ed. Nahum N. Glatzer. London: Vintage Classics, 2005.

Oldenburg, Veena Talwar. "Lifestyle as Resistance: The Case of the Courtesans of Lucknow, India." *Feminist Studies* 16. 2 (Speaking for Others/Speaking for Self: Women of Color) (Summer, 1990): 259–87. Web. 30 May 2012. <http://links.jstor.org/sici?sici=0046-3663%28199022%2916%3A2%3C259%3ALARTCO%3E2.0.CO%3B2-A>.

Ruswa, Mirza Mohammad Hadi. *Umrao Jan Ada: Courtesan of Lucknow.* Trans. David Matthews. New Delhi: Rupa & Co., 2007.

Sharar, Abdul Halim, Rosie Llewellyn-Jones, and Veena Talwar Oldenburg. *The Lucknow Omnibus.* USA: Oxford University Press, 2001.

"Stereotypes of Women." Web. 30 May 2012 <ahref="http://encyclopedia.jrank.org/articles/pages/845/Women-Stereotypes-of.html">Women, Stereotypes of</a>.

"Tawaif." Web. 30 May 2012 <http://en.wikipedia.org/wiki/Tawaif>.

CONCLUSION

The imagined erotic value attached to the cult of the courtesan and their "siren-like" existence might seem to make a comfortable pair. Many colonial and postcolonial notions and ideas have been instrumental in outlining the ways of studying the courtesan culture. It becomes significant, therefore, to attempt to study the cult of the courtesan devoid of any critical influences and pejorative discourses. The British interests were visible with trade that gradually went on to force its governance on the local people of India. The formation of the East India Company in 1600 sealed India's fate for the next hundred years. Since the beginning of the seventeenth century, Northern India witnessed major political and cultural upheavals that culminated in the Mutiny of 1857. The acceptance of the local Indian women into British households was also mistaken as a welcome hybridity. This assimilation could have given rise to a new set of ideas about gender, class and race that seemingly penetrated British-Indian households. The act of maintaining concubines and harems in "colonial families" gave native women the right to a nominal economic inheritance that was decided by the British officials. These "conjugal units" of interracial and sexual exchanges were not bound by marriage. The British officials not only adopted the Indian way of dressing up for social gathering but also took interest in "native" cultural activities, food and styles. Such acclimatization made possible the existence of harem-like arrangements within the British households making it a part of their convenient colonial agenda that silently pronounced the vulnerabilities of such cultural assimilations.

Around the late eighteenth century, Lucknow saw the overarching presence of the kotha culture that improved the interaction between court nawabs, kings and their involvement with the courtesan culture. In the eighteenth century, these kothas also gained mobility with deredar tawaifs who performed in tents for military patrons. This shift from the kotha that was permanently situated within the city to a kotha that was made mobile due to passionate preferences of kings and Nawabs reflect on the growing prosperity of the arts. The courtesans of Lucknow saw patrons who were the followers of the courtesan's arts that consisted of extensive knowledge of literature, their proficiency in music and musicology, dance and their *ada*.

From the time that official data is available, tawaifs are the only women listed as property owners and the only ones paying income tax. The encampment had not been entirely abandoned because the notional connection to the original deredars was of extreme importance for these women. However, the more permanent *kotha*, or the first floor salon, became the new home for the singing ladies. They were, however, ready to leave its comforts for the right offer but never travelled unescorted. (Kidwai, 3)

This reflects deeply on the economy that helped this culture flourish. The cadence of Urdu poetry, erudite musings on Persian and Urdu texts and the performative skills of dance and music blended into Kathak recitals which were abundant in Lucknow in terms of its consumption. The deterioration in the perception of such arts started with the British interpretation of the mehfil. Their problems with understanding the Indian languages and their underlying poetic meanings, led to their calling it as "'nautch' (from Hindi *nach*, i.e, dance)" (Gordon, 318). This was one such problem amongst other problems. For example, the growing threat of interracial marriages that made their racial purity vulnerable.

The late twentieth century saw severe licensing and policing on performances and the shutting down of kothas was carried out massively post the Mutiny. Local traders and propertied class, who were the new propertied class and had mercantile wealth, started moving into elite gatherings of the kotha. The kotha that earlier observed strict decorum and entertained a limited gathering per performance was now getting a more dispersed audience who did not have the patience for understanding the nuances of the kotha structure. The same has been pictured vividly in Farooqi's *Between Clay and Dust* and *Umrao Jan Ada*. However, with the spread of mercantile wealth, several "untutored wealthy men" (Gordon, 318) began to visit the kotha. The emergence of such a clientele can be also read as an ushering of the twilight of Awadh's rich and sophisticated culture. This brought in the issues of "reform and nationalism" (Gordon, 318) glimpses of which can be seen in Ruswa's *Umrao Jan Ada*. In 1893, the Viceroy of Madras and the Excellencies of other states such as Lucknow and Calcutta, passed a memorial that solicited the support of people in removing the "evil practices" (Nevile, 118) of the nautch. It said:

1. That there exists in the Indian community a class of women commonly known as nautch-girls.
2. That these women are invariably prostitutes.
3. That countenance and encouragement are given to them, and even a recognised status in society secured to them, by the practice which prevails among Hindus,

to a very undesirable extent, of inviting them to take part in marriage and other festivities, and even to entertainments given in honor of guests who are not Hindus.

4. That this practice not only necessarily lowers the moral tone of society, but also tends to destroy that family life on which national soundness depends, and to bring upon individuals ruin in property and character alike.

5. That this practice rests only upon fashion, and receives no authority from antiquity or religion, and accordingly has no claim to be considered a National Institution, and is entitled to no respect as such.

...

6. That your Memorialists accordingly appeal to Your Excellency, as the official and recognised head of society in the Presidency of Madras, and as the representative of Her Most Gracious Majesty, the Queen-Empress, in whose influence and example he cause of purity has ever found support, to discourage this pernicious practice by declining to attend any entertainment at which nautch-girls are invited to perform, and thus to strengthen the hands of those who are

> trying to purify the social life of their
> community.
>
> (Nevile, 119–120)

Such notions of strict reform and nationalism crushed the spirit of tawaifdom and the most visible change that the kotha saw was the change of perceiving entertainment and arts of the audiences. According to Oldenburg's essay "Lifestyle as Resistance," the usual power structure operated on the basis of the courtesan's preferences:

> The courtesan in turn had to comply with patron's preferences in performance, but she could exercise control over proceedings and also over who should be admitted to the performance. Control, finally enabled courtesans to have family members live in their establishments, especially daughters, real or putative, who could become singers, but also sons and brothers who attended to service tasks and even served as subsidiary musical accompanists.
>
> (Gordon and Feldman, 318)

This new setup of choice that changed the ways of the courtesan way of life that were to act according to the changing tastes if the patrons, compelled them to eliminate dance recitals from their performances or limit it due to time constraints. Later day licensing also

134

include moderation on the common man's association with courtesans and any sort of liaison with them led to social condemnation. The power structure, therefore, shifted outside the purview of the ways of life of the courtesan. This was replaced by the publicly-held stage performances for the masses. Therefore, with the colonial agenda, came the conscious replacement from privately held performances that symbolized the preferences of the elite to performances held in large public gatherings. In the introduction of *The Courtesan's Arts*, Martha Feldman and Bonnie Gordon write:

> In India...the postcolonial, modernizing process did not take place until the mid-twentieth century. When it did, the quasi-feudal patronage system for courtesans entered a phase of rapid demise. But a new kind of postmodern court, created through the global market of grassroots cassette industries and the festivalization phenomenon of which... has now emerged for those descendants of courtesans who still make their traditional art, allowing at least some tawa'if to speak in the public sphere to an extraordinarily wide audience. (Feldman and Gordon, 14)

This bears recall on the commercialization of music and arts that transformed a kotha-specific experience into the drawing-room culture. The above extract highlights the degeneration of the tawaifdom in two levels: the "festivalization" process that it had to adapt to, and the subsequent pejorative meanings it was attached to. The kotha offered the cpurtesan to showcase the arts in which they were conditioned rigorously and the bygone Mughal era believed in strongly. During the 1920s, the courtesan culture had already faced a death knell and very few courtesans could perform publicly with the consent of the newly formed bourgeoisie or in marriage ceremonies of the people. However, in such a setup, the reason for Begum Akhtar's popularity in this modernized space where an hour-long *raga* could be fit into a 120 mm Shellac record, and could be bought and heard by the public in their respective drawing rooms and spaces without the actual presence of the courtesan, did call for a compromise in the arts of the courtesanship. Begum Akhtar (b. circa. 1914– d. 1974), formerly known as Akhtaribai Faizabadi, did encounter "an extraordinarily wide audience" (quote cited above) and gained prominence in the twentieth century. She is, undoubtedly, called as the "last courtesan," who made such a noticeable mark even during the changing phase of history. The demise of the courtesan culture also can be marked with her progress in the cultural domain as well as in the personal front when she marries Barrister Ishtiaq Ahmed Abbasi of Lucknow. She did merge well with the "grass root cassette industries" (quote cited above) only to produce some of the most haunting light classical expressions of music ever.

It may be worthwhile to talk about similar inclinations toward systems of cultural entertainments in other countries and the manner in which history treats such modes of existence. The Japanese geisha could make for a pertinent discussion. This is because it has managed to maintain its stronghold, core value-system and the grandeur attached to it dis-allowing it to fade away in the pages of history. *The Courtesan's Arts* state:

> In Japan, by contrast, both courtesans and geisha have worked within carefully confined pleasure quarters. In the Edo period (1603-1867), connoisseurs of courtesans gained access to them in the Yoshiwara (or "New Yoshiwara")—the so-called Floating World—through a long boat journey that enacted a ritual transmigration to a space both physically and metaphorically far away from the real world of the city, and hence a transformation of their visitors. (Feldman and Gordon, 14)

Originating in the eighteenth century, the geisha culture literally categorized women who offered pleasure and were known as "entertainers" (Feldman and Gordon, 223).

> The word *gei-sha* literally means "arts person." The courtesans of the pleasure quarters

137

(known as *tayu* in seventeenth- and eighteenth-century Kyoto and *oiran* in eighteenth- and nineteenth-century Edo [Tokyo]) offered their bodies as currency—though very often at a price too high for all but the wealthiest and most popular men to afford. The geisha conversely were defined as selling music, singing and dancing. (Downer, 223)

Japanese geisha, unlike the tawaifs of Lucknow, were clear about their roles as entertainers. The act of selling sex for money was, and still is though much less prominently, not kept under the wraps of art. Even though the geishas were trained in performing arts such as singing, dancing and theatricality the purpose of the act of being a geisha was defined precisely on the basis of offering of sex for money. However, the only difference that demarcated the life of a geisha in Japan was their courtesan's ability to create sexual fantasies as a part of sexual favours for their clients. Japan's Nightless City is one of the best examples that will help us comprehend the geisha society better. The Nightless City was a walled and a gated city that housed around three thousand geishas, courtesans and prostitutes. The city was lined with royal banquets and elegant restaurants where men and women revelled in music, dance, wine and food. "They were entertained by beautiful and charming women with whom, if they were lucky, they might be able to enjoy a sexual encounter... The top ranks of courtesans were at liberty to choose whether or not they slept with their suitors. Men often ruined themselves trying to win their favours" (Downer, *The Courtesan's Arts*, 228). The principles on which the tawaifs of Lucknow operate and the geishas work on nearly resemble each other to a great extent on this level of inquiry. As pointed out by Sharar and Oldenburg, the courtesan way of life followed a hierarchy that stratified the level and the quality of work each courtesan did, the last being the *domni*s who sold bodily pleasures for money and exhibited no art or grace about their profession. Similarly, in Edo Japan, the geisha culture observed strict gradation of ranking. The hierarchy looked somewhat like this:

1. Gion district geishas
2. Pontocho district geishas
3. Kamishichiken district geishas
4. Gion Higashi district geishas
5. Shimbashi, Kagurazaka, Akasaka and Yoshicho district geishas
6. Asakusa district geishas (the lowest working-class geishas)

As Lesley Downer in the essay "The City Geisha and Their Role in Modern Japan: Anomaly or Artistes?" in *The Courtesan's Arts* insightfully informs the readers:

> In many ways the geisha world is like a photographic negative, the looking-glass

> image of "real" Japan. All the usual rules
> are subverted. It is a topsy-turvy world, not
> surprisingly for the geisha world arose out
> of the pleasure quarters, which were set up
> specifically to provide an escape for men from
> drab everyday life into a colourful alternative
> reality. (Downer, 226)

Even though there are considerable principle similarities in the Indian tawaif and the Japanese geisha, the latter had the life of a courtesan further classified and separated from the profession of the geisha. The courtesans in Japan were known for their beauty but were like "caged birds, literally imprisoned within the walled pleasure quarters" (Downer, 229). Even though the courtesans in Japan could exercise monopoly on sex, their freedom was restricted to the gated city. On the other hand, the geishas were not as heavily dressed as the multi-layered kimonos of the courtesans. The geishas wore simple hairstyles and moved freely around the city. "A courtesan wore her huge obi (cummerbund) tied in a huge knot in front of her, implying that it might be untied if a man was lucky and wealthy enough. Geisha conversely were a small obi, tied at the back, like ordinary townswoman" (Downer, 229). The art of dressing elaborately in Japan and India seem similar yet again that reflect on the way the geishas and the tawaifs wore clothes as a visual demarcation from the domestic and married women.

Downer's research interestingly points out that the geishas of Japan could obtain two different licenses—one for entertainment and one for prostitution. This made them Japan's first modern women who could also marry. But marriage was only possible with outcastes such as kabuki actors or sumo wrestlers who came from the domain of the entertainment industry. It can be inferred that the figure of the tawaif, geisha, or courtesan cannot be truly liberated as a woman figure in terms of the choices they have and the extent to which they can exercise it. One does expect some sort of licensing or external restrictions being placed on them.

Also, as Downer states, the becoming of a geisha or choosing this profession could be done in two different ways: being born in a geisha house or parents selling the child for some money and the child growing up into a geisha to repay their debts. So, it can be deciphered that the life of a geisha could be lived either by place of birth or by their parent's decision. Both these cases resemble the Indian way of tawaifdom and resonates the fact that it was inflicted on women either by fate or by birth. Therefore, Umrao's abduction explains the nature of the courtesan way of life. Apart from that, learning the geisha arts is a lifetime dedication to study and perfect the nuances which can be again paralleled with the intensive training in arts, music, dance and literature that the Indian courtesans undergo as a part of their arts. The perfection is achieved when the geisha becomes a living work of art when clubbed with elaborate makeup and skilled artistic capabilities. This applies to the chic culture of the Lucknavi courtesan as well.

Despite several similar traits between the two cultures of "entertainers," one is bound to think of the cultural differences and explore as to what makes geishas survive today and what explains the vanishing culture of the Indian courtesan culture. The courtesan culture in Lucknow seemed to have gained momentum in the 1800s continuing up till the end of the twentieth century. On the other hand, around the 1920s, the geisha culture was at its peak.

> There were about 80,000 geisha throughout Japan including 10, 000 in Tokyo alone. Since the war, however, the options available to both Japanese women (who might once have become geisha) and to Japanese men (who would have been their customers) have much increased. Today there are only 4—5,000 geishas in the whole of Japan…. The final blow was the outlawing of licensed prostitution in 1958—though geisha, who were not considered to be prostitutes, were not outlawed. Thereafter, if sex occurred it was a private matter. (Downer, 231)

The courtesan culture in Japan has practically faded out and tracing women who still practice the arts of the courtesan culture can be difficult in Japan. Lesley Downer makes an important observation during this discourse on the cult of the geishas.

> In order to survive a profession in the modern world, geisha have had to reshape their public image to accord with contemporary notions of propriety. Geisha will tell you that their job has nothing to do with sex; a prime example is Mineko Iwasaki's *Autobiography of a Geisha*. But this is not exactly true. They are not prostitutes in the sense that they have no need to sell themselves cheap. But their profession certainly includes an erotic edge. (Downer, 231)

This concept-based approach can be perfectly applied to the Indian model of tawaifdom who were renowned for their skill in arts, dance, music, literature and as adept entertainers. They were well-versed with the art of teasing and flirtation as well that did not only depend on providing sexual services to the clients. The factors that sustain the cult of the geisha even today will be explored further. Firstly, if one revisits the Downer-quote that says that the geisha world can be called as a "photographic negative of Japan," this becomes the prime reason for the sustenance of the geisha arts. Japan as a nation was not affected by the Judeo-Christian concept of sin and sinning[21]. The use of the word *kabuku* (meaning wild and outrageous) and the emergence of the *kabuki* arts that the geishas mastered, there was no inhibition of being sexual or displaying sexual instincts. On the same lines, Japan was known for its male brothels and also provided consent on male-on-male intercourse. This was taken as a shock by the Westerners in the eighteenth century and Japan faced bans on the operation on male brothels. Downer observes:

> Only men were expected to feel romantic affection. Apart from youths, the other suitable objects of a man's affection were

---

21 The Calvinistic principle (1509) and the Judaic understanding of Law was the law that governed the universe. It incorporated terms and beliefs such as Divine, Sin, Transgression and Punishment. The idea of the Sin laid heavy emphasis on the materiality of the body and soul that was almost like a Scum. Therefore, a beautiful and a pure soul would be face union with God and, the material soul would be bestial (in terms of eating, masticating etc), scum-like and unaccommodating. Calvinism also charted out the path for an apocalyptic moment where one can escape from sins by confessing and repenting near the Alter. Countries like Geneva, Europe, England, South Africa, Germany, and Sweden were affected by this principle. India was affected by it with the setting up of the Presbyterian Church around the 1790s.

> prostitutes, courtesans, geisha, or other inhabitants of the demimonde—the pleasure quarters. It was highly inappropriate for a man to feel or express affection towards non-"professional" women such as his wife. (Downer, 227)

This model of displaying love to other women except the wife of the house is an absolute inversion to the Western and the Indian model. The wives in Japan seem to be a portrayal of emotion-less stoic women who do not wish to sustain their marital liaison on the concept of love. On the other hand, women who became professional geisha or courtesans knew the arts of showing love to the opposite gender. Downer quotes from Naomi Tamura's *The Japanese Bride* (1904):

> It is very clear that we do not marry for love. If a man is known to have broken this rule, we look upon him as a mean fellow, and sadly lacking in morality. His own mother and father would be ashamed of him. Public sentiment places love for a woman very low in the scale of morals…. We place love and brutal attachment on the same plane. (227)

The concept of amorous love therefore does not lead to the marital domain in the Japanese culture. On the contrary, the Judeo-Christian guilt touched the face of Mughal rule only with the incoming of the British colonizers who saw the "excesses" and the "sin" that was involved in unmonitored sexual indulgences and eroticism. This can be the primary factor that Japan did not face the threat of Geisha extinction as rapidly as Indian courtesans did. The cult of the geisha still exists though it might not be in its absolute glory. Geisha arts also tell us that the cult might get extinct in the near future. The prime reason for geishas facing the threat of extinction is not because they have a dying audience but they are lacking skilled musicians and geishas who have the potential to master the art. Geishas were working class girls who chose this profession either out of choice or were sold off to geisha homes for money. The selling off of girls is not considered to be a taboo in Japan. "[R]ather it was a way of providing a girl from a disadvantaged background with a chance in life" (Downer, 231). Does this mean that the Judeo-Christian principle was as strong as its influence on the Oriental was enough to wipe off self-sustaining cultures? The Mughal era certainly did not have access to or the belief to accommodate such Puritanic thoughts within the culture that centrally conceptualized and propagated free love.

The ways of life of the courtesans in Lucknow, as discussed in the chapters, saw intensive schooling in arts, music, dance and Persian literature that surpassed the mere erotic quality attached to the courtesans in modern studies and interpretations. Therefore, it can be safely said that their existence was not corrosive to the Mughal culture but was necessary for its sustenance, networking and prosperity. In this case, Kenneth Clarke's interpretation that Sharar quietly subscribes to in the introductory chapter of *The Lucknow Omnibus* (that a civilization does get exhausted when it reaches its peak of prosperity) proves insufficient somehow. For tawaifdom to have sustained, it is arguably necessary for the culture to have a continued patron-ship and flourishing. Even though Japan did not face severe licensing and moral policing like Lucknow did post the Mutiny phase, the arts could have sustained on its own if the arts were practiced with meticulousness. The courtesan way of life does share a large piece of its sustenance on followers and patrons, but then the entire school of thought, as propagated by Ruswa's *Umrao Jan Ada* and other historians who record and simplify the complex culture of the Lucknow courtesans, do mention and give a specific mention on the musicians and the *maulvi*s who sculpted the courtesan figure out of a regular woman. It can be said had the perpetrator of the arts, irrespective of they being the patriarchs, existed then the cult of the courtesan might not have faded into the historical horizon so violently. The geisha cult in Japan exists for the same reason—Shamisen flute players. Shamisen is the art of playing the flute and it takes years to master the art like any other instrument like the piano or the violin. "But only a veteran can play the shamisen with precision, confidence, and passion" (Downer, 235). Proficient Shamisen players lack in Japan today as not many people find this traditional art worthy of being learnt. Years of practice and dedication can be one of the prime reasons due to this decline. Therefore, the declining geisha culture is pivotalized on the decline of skilled Shamisen players who add erotic quality to the geisha arts.

> This in itself is a threat to the continuation of the geisha world. There are of course plenty of non-geisha players of the shamisen— amateur men and also women and also men; but traditionally the geisha world is a closed community. For the geisha their profession is a calling and a lifestyle, not simply a job. It would be very alien to employ someone from outside the community.
>
> (Downer, 235)

Apart from that, the geisha teahouse parties are very similar to the nautch parties that Begum Samru held and the *mehfil*s that hosted *daawats* for their patrons. These meetings over food were given prime importance that acted as the space for political discussions and discussions of the state apart from sharing literary insights. Due to the decline in the arts of the geisha and the artistes who were associated with it, geisha arts as a consequence, have seen a considerable loss of patrons who no longer find it interesting and refined. The decline in the appreciation of arts is visible. The geishas too face the danger of being highly eroticized but are still considerably distant from getting extinct. Downer records with confidence that Japan still has plenty of women who wish to become geishas attracted by the power and wealth that this class of women can emanate. "To entertain in a teahouse is also the ultimate sign of status, power and wealth" (Downer, 241). The geisha culture sustains the industry of kimono manufacturers, *kabuki* theatre artists, silk weavers, and wooden clogs and wigs. Therefore, Japan cannot afford to lose this link with their tradition. Tawaifdom could have existed in similar lines and worked out a parallel existence to work its future within the seams of modernity. With the version of history available to us it is not very hard to imagine the sounds of musicians playing light classical music within the walls of the Old Fort today. The setting of the *mehfil* and the daring voice of the courtesan piercing the walls of the room as well as the hearts of several keen listeners is a desire that this cult leaves us with even today.

Let this conclusion be a *modus vivendi*[22] to differing opinions and opinions that we agree to disagree. The cult of the courtesan is a discussion that must extend beyond the scope of this study and be studied with reference to

---

[22] John Gray's work around *modus vivendi* signifies the way of living together accommodating disputing thoughts and agreeable thoughts in one body of belief. *Modus* means mode and *vivendi* means living that takes into account temporary and informal arrangements in political affairs. Therefore, this Latin phrase signifies an agreement between differing opinions or opinions of people who "agree to disagree."

cross-cultural arts that sustained similar Spectacles. It is true that the structures of tawaifdom continue to inhabit the modern society but with a lot of degeneration and euphemisms. Modern day struggle for sex-related ideas and gender queries have launched itself within movements such as LGBT movement, queer movements or the Gay Bombay movement. This has indeed sensitized the masses and provided a space that has improved the interaction supporting the legalization of prostitution in India or gay rights in the country. But the courtesan's arts and their way of life, as it existed, cannot be discussed within the same space. As the argument goes prostitution in India and otherwise is spoken in terms of the "politics of exclusion" that demarcates the social space from the private space of the sex-workers. This politics of exclusion groups and regroups same-sex love or prostitution as a subsect that must have its space within mainstream society. Courtesanship, on the other hand, cannot fit into the argument as it was the mainstream culture in itself rather than being a part of it. The courtesans were closely affiliated with court politics and influenced the decisions of the court and its proceedings. They were a body of knowledge that helped the sons of nawabs gain *adab* and literary insights that the Mughal culture strongly believed in. While today we study the politics in prostitution and related issues, the courtesans studied the politics of the Age. The West must not always be vilified. The extinction also cannot be explained with the lack of patron-ship. According to a theory derived by Anthony Giddens, the society only has forms which can show its symptoms on the people living in it. As one form replaces the other, the people too adjust to the change or make necessary changes to the structure of society. It is sad that tawaifdom as a form remains only to get affected by the changing structures of society. This shows that the arts of the courtesans have not completely died. People are still in the process of *modus vivendi*.

Works Cited

Farooqi, Musharaff Ali. *Between Clay and Dust.* Trans. David Davidar. New Delhi: Aleph Book Company, 2012.

Feldman, Martha and Bonnie Gordon. *The Courtesan's Arts: Cross-cultural Perspectives.* USA: Oxford University Press, 2006.

Feldman, Martha and Bonnie Gordon. *The Courtesan's Arts: Cross-cultural Perspectives.* USA: Oxford University Press, 2006.

Kidwai, Saleem. "The Singing Ladies Find a Voice." Web. <http://www.india-seminar.com/2004/540/540%20 saleem%20kidwai.htm>.

"Modus Vivendi." Web. 30 May 2012 <http://en.wikipedia. org/wiki/Modus_vivendi>.

Neville, Pran. *Nautch Girls of the Raj.* Delhi: Penguin, 2009.

Sharar, Abdul Halim, Rosie Llewellyn-Jones, and Veena Talwar Oldenburg. *The Lucknow Omnibus.* USA: Oxford University Press, 2001.

BIBLIOGRAPHY

"Off Modern: A Conversation with Raqs." Web. 30 May 2012 <http://humanitiesunderground.wordpress.com/category/performative/>.

"Plutocracy." Web. 30 May 2012 <http://en.wikipedia.org/wiki/Plutocracy>.

"Tawaif." Web. 30 May 2012 <http://en.wikipedia.org/wiki/Tawaif>.

A Lady's Diary of the Siege of Lucknow. Delhi: Rupa & Co., 2002.

Ali, Kamran Asdar. "Courtesans in the Living Room." *ISIM Review* No. 15 (2005).

Armstrong, Karen. *Islam: A Short History*. Great Britain: Phoenix, 2009.

Baig, Mirza Farhatullah. The Last Mushaira of Dehli. Trans. Akhtar Qamber. New Delhi: Orient Blackswan, 2010.

Chakravarty, Gautam. *The Indian Mutiny and the British Imagination*. Delhi: Cambridge, 2005.

Chattopadhyay, Bankimchandra. *The Poison Tree*. Trans. Marian Maddern and S. N. Mukherjee. Delhi: Penguin, 1996.

Clark, Kenneth. *Civilisation*. London: BBC Books, 1969.

Connerney, Richard D. "The X-rated Newsletter or Donkeys Don't Smile: Sex and Love in India." *ICWA Letters (South Asia)*. Web. 30 May 2012. <http://susiebright.blogs.com/Donkeys_Dont_Smile.pdf>.

Dalrymple, William. *White Mughals*. India: Penguin, 2004.

Dewey, Susan. *Hollow Bodies: Institutional Responses to Sex Trafficking in Armenia*, Bosnia and India. Virginia: Kumarian, 2008.

Eraly, Abraham. *The Mughal World*. Delhi: Eastern Book Corporation, 2007.

Faraone, Christopher A., and Laura K. McClure, ed. *Prostitutes and Courtesans in the Ancient World the University of Wisconsin Press*. Wisconsin: Monroe Street Madison, 2006. Web. 30 May 2012. <https://mail-attachment.googleusercontent.com/attachment/?ui=2&ik=c3570a1086&view=att&th=1374c19fab09c a1c&attid=0.9&disp=inline&realattid=f_h27f3xc112 &safe=1&zw&saduie=AG9B_P9KWrpXVNjYBltK KGhqF_4b&sadet=1338227823797&sads=1BVso2Iw 5tEg1o5i5u5i7vZ4A08>.

Farooqi, Musharaff Ali. *Between Clay and Dust*. Trans. David Davidar. New Delhi: Aleph Book Company, 2012.

Faruqi, Shamshur Rehman. *The Flower-lit Road: Essays in Urdu Literary Theory and Criticism*. Stanford: Laburnum Press, 2005.

Feldman, Martha and Bonnie Gordon. *The Courtesan's Arts: Cross-cultural Perspectives*. USA: Oxford University Press, 2006.

Genet, Jean. *The Balcony*. Ed. B. Mangalam. Delhi: Worldview Publications, 2005

Ghosh, Durba. *Sex and the Family in Colonial India: The Making of Empire*. Cambridge: Cambridge University Press, 2006.

Gregory D. Booth. "Making a Woman from a Tawaif: Courtesans as Heroes in Hindi Cinema." *New Zealand Journal of Asian Studies* 9. 2 (2007): 1–26. Web. <http://www.nzasia.org.nz/downloads/NZJAS-%20 Dec07/02Booth6.pdf>.

Hunt, Lynn. *Eroticism and the Body Politic*. London: Johns Hopkins University Press, 1992.

Illustrated Oxford English Dictionary. India: DK Publishers Illustration and OUP Publication, 2003.

Jackson, Brian L. "The Harem Syndrome.' PARRC Research, Inc. 2006. Web. 30 May 2012. <http:// www.pdfnow.net/pdf/the-harem-syndrome.html>.

Jain, Jasbir. *Indigenous Roots of Feminism: Culture, Subjectivity and Agency*. Delhi: SAGE, 2011.

Kafka, Franz. *The Complete Short Stories*. Ed. Nahum N. Glatzer. London: Vintage Classics, 2005.

Kidwai, Saleem. "The Singing Ladies Find a Voice." Web. <http://www.india-seminar.com/2004/540/540%20 saleem%20kidwai.htm>.

Lal, K. S. *The Mughal Harem*. New Delhi: Aditya Prakashan, 1992.

Lal, Vinay. "The Courtesan and the Indian Novel." *Indian Literature* 139 (Sep.–Oct. 1995): 164–70.

Llewellyn-Jones, Rosie. *Engaging Scoundrels: True Tales of Old Lucknow*. Delhi: Oxford University Press, 1999.

Markel, Stephen and Tushara Bindu Gude. "India's Fabled City—The Art of Courtly Lucknow. Los Angeles County Museum of Art. Web. 30 May 2012. <http://www.lacma.org/art/exhibition/ indias-fabled-city-art-courtly-lucknow>.

Matthews, David, trans. *Umrao Jan Ada*. New Delhi, Rupa and Co., 2006

Maulana Ashraf Ali Thanvi. Introduction. *Bihishti Zewar* (Special Edition). India: DK Publishers Illustration and OUP Publication, 2003, p. 775.

Misra, Amaresh. *Lucknow: Fire of Grace—The Story of its Renaissance, Revolution and the Aftermath*. India: Harper Collins Publishers, 1998.

Nath, R. Private Life of the Mughals of India (1526–1803 A.D.). Delhi: Rupa, 2007.

Neville, Pran. *Nautch Girls of the Raj.* Delhi: Penguin, 2009.

Oldenburg, Veena Talwar. "Lifestyle as Resistance: The Case of the Courtesans of Lucknow, India." *Feminist Studies* 16. 2 (Speaking for Others/Speaking for Self: Women of Color) (Summer, 1990): 259–87. Web. 30 May 2012. <http://links.jstor.org/sici?sici=0046-3663%28199022%2916%3A2%3C259%3ALARTC O%3E2.0.CO%3B2-A>.

Pritchett, Frances W. *Nets of Awareness: Urdu Poetry and its Critics.* California: University of California Press, 1994.

Ruswa, Mirza Mohammad Hadi. *Umrao Jan Ada: Courtesan of Lucknow.* Trans. David Matthews. New Delhi: Rupa & Co., 2007.

Sahni, Rohini. *Prostitution and Beyond: An Analysis of Sex Workers in India.* New Delhi: SAGE, 2008.

Sampath, Vikram. *"My Name is Gauhar Jaan!" The Life and Times of a Musician.* New Delhi: Rupa, 2010.

Shah, Hasan. *The Nautch Girl: A Novel*. Trans. Qurratulain Hyder. New Delhi: Sterling Publishers, 1992.

Shah, Hasan. *The Nautch Girl: A Novel*. Trans. Qurratulain Hyder. New Delhi: Sterling Publishers, 1992.

Sharar, Abdul Halim, Rosie Llewellyn-Jones, and Veena Talwar Oldenburg. *The Lucknow Omnibus*. USA: Oxford University Press, 2001.

Sharma, Partap. *Begum Sumroo: A Play in Three Acts*. Delhi: Rupa & Co., 2007.

Shreeve, Nicholas. *Dark Legacy: The Fortunes of Begam Samru*. Calcutta: Rupa & Co., 1998.

Spivak, Gayatri Chakravorty. *Conversations with Gayatri Chakravorty Spivak*. Calcutta: Seagull Books, 2006.

Stark, Ulrike. "Politics, Public Issues and the Promotion of Urdu Literature: Avadh Akhbar, the First Urdu Daily in Northern India." The Annual of Urdu Studies 18. 1 (2003): 66–94.

Taneja, Anand Vivek. "Begum Samru atrivedind the Security Guard." Web. 30 May 2012. <www.sarai. net/publications/readers/05-bare-acts/04_anand. pdf>.

Taylor, Philip Meadows. *Confessions of a Thug.* Delhi: Rupa, 2001.

Thanvi, Maulana Ashraf Ali. *Bihishti Zewar* (Special Edition). Trans. Barbara Daly Metcalf. California: University Of California Press, 1992.

Tharu, Susie and K. Lalita, ed. *Women Writing in India: 600 BC to the Present, Volume 1.* Delhi: Oxford University Press, 1991.

Trivedi, Madhu. *The Making of the Awadh Culture.* New Delhi: Primus Books, 2010.

ABOUT THE AUTHOR

Aditi Dasgupta, an explorer guided by deep sense of intellectual enquiry, completed her M.Phil. in English. Her area of academic interest lies in postcolonial literature and comprehending problems of identity and nationality. Aditi has been associated with organizations like Times Group, Adfactors PR and Mahindra & Mahindra.